Economic Feasibility of Projects

ECONOMIC FEASIBILITY OF PROJECTS

Managerial and Engineering Practice

Third Edition

S. L. Tang

Civil & Structural Engineering Department
The Hong Kong Polytechnic University

The Chinese University Press

Economic Feasibility of Projects: Managerial and Engineering Practice, Third edition

By S.L. Tang

© **The Chinese University of Hong Kong**, 2003

ISBN 962-996-115-6

Previous editions © McGraw-Hill Book Co., Singapore, 1996, 1991

THE CHINESE UNIVERSITY PRESS

The Chinese University of Hong Kong
SHA TIN, N.T., HONG KONG

Fax: +852-2603 6692, +852-2603 7355
E-mail: cup@cuhk.edu.hk
Web-site: www.chineseupress.com

Printed in Hong Kong

Contents

Preface to the Third Edition

This is a textbook for engineering and business/management undergraduates and postgraduate students and a reference for practicing engineers or managers who are familiar with their projects but less familiar with financial/economic analysis methods. It is also suitable for self-study, as there are not many similar books in the market.

The book is divided into two parts. Part 1 consists of six chapters and covers all the basic concepts and theories, providing the readers with a good understanding of the financial and economic analysis on the feasibility of projects. It includes discussions on the time value of money, internal rate of return and net present worth, effect of inflation, comparison of multiple alternatives, and financial versus economic appraisals. The contents are developed logically to adequate breath and depth for most applications of project feasibility studies. Plenty of examples are used to illustrate the theories, arguments and calculations.

Part 2 consists of two chapters which are case studies on both financial and economic feasibility studies. These case studies complement well the theories discussed in Part 1. Readers should be able to conduct their own financial and economic analyses by following the procedures and methodology of the examples given.

A wide range of different types of projects is used as examples in the book. Readers may benefit from going through the examples, which are interesting introduction to the arguments and theories, and may also provide them with a glimpse of real projects. It is hope that this book will equip its readers with sufficient skills to handle their project feasibility studies.

The previous editions of the book have been well-received. In this third edition, the chapters have been revised and expanded with the latest theories and data added, especially the most up-dated information on the development of the theories of internal rate of return and net present worth.

The author wishes to thank all those who have helped in the preparation of this edition, and to The Chinese University Press for publishing the book.

S. L. Tang

May 2003

Part I

THEORIES

1. Time Value of Money

1.1 Introduction

If you were lucky enough to win a prize of $100,000 from a lucky draw and were asked to choose to have this money today or to have it a year later, what would you choose?

This question sounds a bit silly because everybody's answer will of course be to get it today. The reasons are obvious for not wanting to have it a year later, just to name a few:

(a) Growth of money: Extra money can be earned by properly investing the $100,000 so that this sum of money will grow and become a larger sum a year later.

(b) Inflation: The purchasing power of $100,000 a year later will decline.

(c) Risk: There is a chance of being unable to receive the $100,000 a year later due to the possibility of something unexpected happening in the year.

The growth of money, as described in (a) above, is usually referred to as the *time value of money*. It is normally expressed as a percentage in a definite period, e.g. 10% per annum (or i% p.a. in general), and reflects the *rate of return* of the sum of money if the latter is properly invested. It should not be confused with the rate of inflation, which is normally expressed as f% p.a. The following section will further explain and distinguish the effects of inflation and the time value of money.

1.2 Apparent Rate of Return and Real Rate of Return

Assuming that $100,000 is invested in a good business in 1994 and it grows to $125,000 in 1995 and then to $150,000 in 1996. This is represented by the bold line in Fig. 1.1.

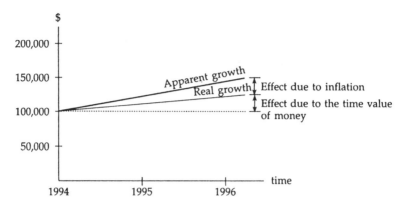

Fig. 1.1 Growth of money vs. time.

It must be noted that the value of money in 1996 is lower than that in 1994, that is, the purchasing power of $150,000 of 1996 is less than that of 1994, due to inflation. Therefore, although the money grows in two years from $100,000 to $150,000, the investor suffers at the same time a loss due to the inflation of money in this period. The apparent rate of return, i', is a result of the combined effects of inflation and the time value of money. The real rate of return, i, however, reflects only the time value of money, or more exactly, the real growth of money which indicates the real increase in purchasing power with time. The relationship between i (real rate of return in % p.a.), i' (apparent rate of return in % p.a.) and f (rate of inflation in % p.a.) is:

$$i' = (1 + i)(1 + f) - 1 \tag{1.1}$$

The above equation will be further discussed in Chapter 4. Note that equation (1.2) below is an approximation of equation (1.1) for small values of i and f:

$$i' = i + f \tag{1-2}$$

It should be pointed out that the interest rates quoted by banks are apparent rates. Apparent rates are also called *nominal rates*. If the inflation rate is higher than the interest rate, it would result in a net loss for depositing money in a bank.

1.3 Mathematics of Compound Interest

1.3.1 Introduction

It is important to note that the inflation-free assumption is made in the following discussion up to Chapter 3. This would mean the purchasing power of money will remain unchanged, or in other words, no inflation will take place in the period of time under consideration. This is of course merely an assumption and is usually not true in real life. It is necessary, however, to make this assumption for the time being and it will be brought up again for further discussion and adjustment later in Chapter 4. The interest rate in such a case, therefore, can be regarded as a real rate rather than an apparent rate. Hence, only the effect of the time value of money is considered in the following discussion.

1.3.2 Compound amount factor

Let P = the initial investment or the principal sum
           n = the number of periods, which refers usually to months or years
           i = interest rate in % per period
           S = the total sum of money accumulated after n periods

Compound amount of P after 1 period = $P(1 + i)$
Compound amount of P after 2 periods = $P(1 + i)(1 + i) = P(1 + i)^2$
Compound amount of P after 3 periods = $P(1 + i)^2(1 + i) = P(1 + i)^3$

Similarly,

Compound amount of P after n periods = $P(1 + i)^n$

Or $S = P(1 + i)^n$ (1.3)

Diagrammatically, the relationship can be shown as in Fig. 1.2.

Fig. 1.2 Sum of money accumulated after n periods due to an initial single payment.

The factor $(1 + i)^n$ is called *compound amount factor* (caf) and equation (1.3) can be written as:

$S = P \times (\text{caf})^{n,i}$ (1.4)

The values of $(\text{caf})^{n,i}$ for n = 1 to 30 and i = 1% to 25% are shown in Appendix 1.

Example 1.1

$10,000 is put in a fixed account of a bank offering an interest rate of 8 percent per annum compounded half annually. What will be the compound amount after 5 years?

Solution 1.1

8% per annum compounded half annually for 5 years means 4% per period compounded for 10 periods.
    The compound amount after 5 years
    $= 10{,}000 \times (\text{caf})^{n=10, i=4\%}$
    $= 10{,}000 \times (1.4802)$
    $= \$14{,}802$

Readers are strongly advised at this jucture to do exercise Problem 2 at the end of this chapter before reading further.

1.3.3   Uniform series compound amount factor

Let A = the periodic uniform payment made *at the end of each period* continuing for n periods to accumulate a sum S.
    The situation can be presented diagrammatically as shown in Fig. 1.3.

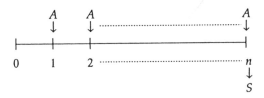

Fig. 1.3 Sum of money accumulated after n periods due to uniform periodic payments.

Compound amount of the first A at period n	$= A(1 + i)^{n-1}$
Compound amount of the second A at period n	$= A(1 + i)^{n-2}$
Compound amount of the third A at period n	$= A(1 + i)^{n-3}$
Compound amount of the $(n-2)$th A at period n	$= A(1 + i)^{2}$
Compound amount of the $(n-1)$th A at period n	$= A(1 + i)^{1}$
Compound amount of the nth A at period n	$= A$
Total	$= S$

Thus $S = A + A(1 + i)^{1} + A(1 + i)^{2} + ...+ A(1 + i)^{n-1}$ (1.5)

Multiplying (1.5) by $(1 + i)$, we obtain:

$$S(1 + i) = A(1 + i)^1 + A(1 + i)^2 + ... + A(1 + i)^n \tag{1.6}$$

Subtracting (1.5) from (1.6), we have:

$$S(1 + i) - S = A(1 + i)^n - A$$

i.e. $S = A\left[\dfrac{(1+i)^n - 1}{i}\right]$ (1.7)

The factor $\left[\dfrac{(1+i)^n - 1}{i}\right]$ is called the *uniform series compound amount*

factor (uscaf) and equation (1.7) can be written as follows:

$$S = A \times (\text{uscaf})^{n,i} \tag{1.8}$$

The values of $(\text{uscaf})^{n,i}$ for $n = 1$ to 30 and $i = 1\%$ to 25% are shown in Appendix 1.

Example 1.2

A manufacturing company will have to replace one of its machines 5 years from now. A new machine costs $125,000. How much is the end-of-year annual installment the company has to put into a bank in order to save enough money in five years to buy the new machine if the bank is offering an interest rate of 8% per annum?

Solution 1.2

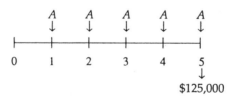

Fig. 1.4 Sum of $125,000 accumulated due to uniform periodic payments.

Note that the machine always costs $125,000, whether now or in five years, as the inflation-free assumption has been made.

$$125,000 = A \times (\text{uscaf})^{n=5, i=8\%}$$
$$= A(5.867)$$
$$\text{or } A = \frac{125,000}{5.867} = \$21,306$$

1.3.4   Uniform series sinking fund factor

The equations (1.7) or (1.8) are a little cumbersome for calculating A, which can be found directly using the following equation, which is obtained by rearranging the terms of equation (1.7):

$$A = S\left[\frac{i}{(1+i)^n - 1}\right] \quad (1.9)$$

The factor $\left[\dfrac{i}{(1+i)^n - 1}\right]$ is called the *uniform series sinking fund factor* (ussff) and equation (1.9) can be expressed in the form below:

$$A = S \times (\text{ussff})^{n,i} \quad (1.10)$$

A in this case is called the *sinking fund*. The values of $(\text{ussff})^{n,i}$ for $n = 1$ to 30 and $i = 1\%$ to 25% are shown in Appendix 1.

Example 1.3

Repeat doing Example 1.2 but use this time $(\text{ussf})^{n,i}$ to calculate A.

Solution 1.3

$$\begin{aligned} A &= 125,000 \times (\text{ussff})^{n=5, i=8\%} \\ &= 125,000 \times (0.17045) \\ &= \$21,306 \end{aligned}$$

We obtain the same answer as in Solution 1.2, of course.

1.3.5   Uniform series capital recovery factor

All previous examples illustrate the relationship between the final accumulated sum and a principal sum investment or an investment in the form of a series of uniform installments. What follows, however, is the discussion of the relationship between the initial loan and the subsequent uniform series of payments to offset against the loan. The situation can be presented diagrammatically as shown in Figure 1.5.

Equation (1.3) gives: $S = P(1 + i)^n$

Also equation (1.7) gives: $S = A\left[\dfrac{(1+i)^n - 1}{i}\right]$

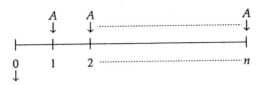

Fig. 1.5 Uniform periodic payments for recovering a loan P.

Eliminating S, we obtain:

$$P(1+i)^n = A\left[\frac{(1+i)^n - 1}{i}\right]$$

i.e. $A = P\left[\dfrac{i(1+i)^n}{(1+i)^n - 1}\right]$ (1.11)

The factor $\left[\dfrac{i(1+i)^n}{(1+i)^n - 1}\right]$ is called the *uniform series capital recovery factor* (uscrf) and equation (1.11) can be written as follows:

$A = P \times (\text{uscrf})^{n,i}$ (1.12)

The values of $(\text{uscrf})^{n,i}$ for $n = 1$ to 30 and $i = 1\%$ to 25% are shown in Appendix 1.

Example 1.4

If the machine of Example 1.3 suddenly breaks down so that the company needs to buy a new one immediately and has to borrow from a bank $125,000 at an interest rate of 8% per annum, what would be the annual installment for repaying the loan in 5 years?

Solution 1.4

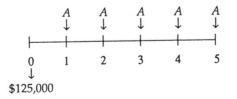

Fig. 1.6 Uniform periodic payments for recovering a loan of $125,000.

$$A = 125{,}000 \times (\text{uscrf})^{n=5, i=8\%}$$
$$= 125{,}000 \times (0.25045)$$
$$= \$31{,}306$$

It interesting to note that the last four digits of the above answer are the same as those of Solution 1.3, which is $21,306. One tends to think that this is merely coincidental but in fact it is not. This apparent coincidence will be explained in detail in Section 5 of this chapter.

Example 1.5

A man wishes to hire-purchase a stereo hifi set which costs $3,600. The down payment required is $300 and the balance will be paid by 12 end-of-period installments, once every month. Calculate the amount of each monthly installment if the interest charged is 24% per annum.

Solution 1.5

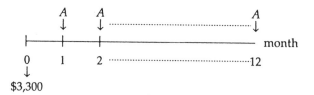

Fig. 1.7 Uniform periodic payments for recovering a loan of $3,300.

Money borrowed = $3,600 – $300 = $3,300
i = 24% p.a. or i = 2% p.m.
A = monthly instalment
$$= 3{,}300 \times (\text{uscrf})^{n=12, i=2\%}$$
$$= 3{,}300 \times (0.09455)$$
$$= \$312$$

1.4 Present Worth

Look at Fig. 1.8, F would be equal to $25,937 if i is taken as 10%. In other words, $25,937 of 10 years from now is equivalent to $10,000 today, or the *present worth* (i.e. today's worth) of $25,937 of ten years later is $10,000. Mathematically, the present worth of F *in general* can be expressed in the form of:

$$\text{Present worth of } F = \frac{F}{(1+i)^n} = F \times \left[\frac{1}{(1+i)^n}\right] \qquad (1.13)$$

Fig. 1.8 Present worth of a single payment F.

The factor $\left[\dfrac{1}{(1+i)^{n}}\right]$ is called the present worth factor (pwf) and equation (1.13) can be written as:

Present worth of $F = F \times (\mathrm{pwf})^{n,i}$ \hfill (1.14)

The values of $(\mathrm{pwf})^{n,i}$ for $n = 1$ to 30 and $i = 1\%$ to 25% are shown in Appendix 1.

Consider a uniform series of payments as shown in Fig. 1.9:

Fig. 1.9 Present worth of uniform periodic payments.

The equivalent sum of money *today,* which is equivalent to all these uniform series of payment for n periods, is called the *present worth* and can be calculated from the equation:

$$\frac{F}{1+i}+\frac{F}{(1+i)^{2}}+\frac{F}{(1+i)^{3}}+\ldots+\frac{F}{(1+i)^{n}}$$

$$= F\left[\frac{(1+i)^{n}-1}{i(1+i)^{n}}\right] \tag{1.15}$$

(The derivation of this is left to the reader.)

The factor $\left[\dfrac{(1+i)^{n}-1}{i(1+i)^{n}}\right]$ is called the *uniform series present worth factor* (uspwf) and equation (1.15) can be written as:

Present worth of n uniform series of payment F

$= F \times (\mathrm{uspwf})^{n,i}$ \hfill (1-16)

The values of (uspwf)^{n,i} for $n = 1$ to 30 and $i = 1\%$ to 25% are shown in Appendix 1.

1.5 The Philosophy of Compound Interest

The basic idea of compound interest is that the interest is calculated *based on the new balance*. If $100 is deposited in a bank and the interest rate is 10% per annum, it becomes $110 (i.e. $100 × 1.10) at the end of the first year. The interest gained in the following year will be calculated based on the *new balance* of $110, and this sum will again grow to $121 (i.e. $110 × 1.10) at the end of the second year. The new balance will at that time be $121 and therefore will grow to $133.10 (i.e. $121 × 1.10) at the end of the third year and so on. The above is the scene in depositing money in a savings account. The same philosophy applies to the interest charged to a loan, that is, interest will be charged based on the *new balance* (or the unpaid balance) of the loan. Let us take a look at several different repayment methods in recovering a loan of $100,000 in 5 years at $i = 10\%$ per annum.

Note: i is sometimes termed the *cost of capital* because one has to pay that amount of money in order to obtain such a capital. In this case, one has to pay $10,000 a year (10%) in order to obtain a loan of $100,000.

Method 1

The principal sum borrowed (i.e. $100,000) be amortized in five years, $20,000 each year, as shown in Table 1.1:

Table 1.1 Uniform principal amortization for a loan of $100,000

End of year	(1) Principal borrowed	(2) Principal amortization	(3) Unpaid balance (i.e. new balance)	(4) Interest charged to new balance (Col 3×10%)	(5) Annual instalment (Col 2 + Col 4)
0	100,000		100,000		
1		20,000	80,000	10,000	30,000
2		20,000	60,000	8,000	28,000
3		20,000	40,000	6,000	26,000
4		20,000	20,000	4,000	24,000
5		20,000	0	2,000	22,000
					130,000

Method 2

The principal sum borrowed be amortized in five years in an increasing manner from $10,000 to $30,000 as per Table 1.2.

Table 1.2 Non-uniform principal amortization for loan $100,000

End of year	(1) Principal borrowed	(2) Principal amortization	(3) Unpaid balance (i.e. new balance)	(4) Interest charged to new balance (Col 3×10%)	(5) Annual instalment (Col 2 + Col 4)
0	100,000		100,000		
1		10,000	90,000	10,000	20,000
2		15,000	75,000	9,000	24,000
3		20,000	55,000	7,500	27,500
4		25,000	30,000	5,500	30,500
5		30,000	0	3,000	33,000
					135,000

It must be noted that the present worths of the annual instalments for both methods are the same. They both equal to $100,000 taking $i = 10\%$ per annum and can be shown mathematically as follows:

Present worth (Method 1)

$$= \frac{30,000}{1+0.1} + \frac{28,000}{(1+0.1)^2} + \frac{26,000}{(1+0.1)^3} + \frac{24,000}{(1+0.1)^4} + \frac{22,000}{(1+0.1)^5}$$

$$= \$100,000$$

Present worth (Method 2)

$$= \frac{20,000}{1+0.1} + \frac{24,000}{(1+0.1)^2} + \frac{27,500}{(1+0.1)^3} + \frac{30,500}{(1+0.1)^4} + \frac{33,000}{(1+0.1)^5}$$

$$= \$100,000$$

Therefore, although the total amount of annual instalment for Method 1 ($130,000) is apparently less than that for Method 2 ($135,000), it would be erroneous to take Method 1 merely because of its lower value of total instalments as a better alternative, since it has been shown above that their present worths are the same.

Now let us look at the third method.

Method 3

The principal sum borrowed to be paid in a lump sum at the end of Year 5 is as shown in Table 1.3.

Table 1.3 Single redempting payment for a loan of $100,000.

End of year	(1) Principal borrowed	(2) Principal amortization	(3) Unpaid balance (i.e. new balance)	(4) Interest charged to new balance (Col 3×10%)	(5) Annual instalment (Col 2 + Col 4)
0	100,000		100,000		
1		0	100,000	10,000	10,000
2		0	100,000	10,000	10,000
3		0	100,000	10,000	10,000
4		0	100,000	10,000	10,000
5		100,000	0	10,000	110,000
					150,000

The present worth of the annual installments for this method will of course be the same again, i.e. $100,000, if i is taken as 10 percent per annum. (The mathematical proof for this is shown in Section 1.6)

The reader's attention is drawn to columns (3) and (4) of Table 1.3. Apparently, the annual interest seems to have been calculated as *simple interest*, giving $10,000 of interest all the time from Year 1 to Year 5. The calculation has been based on the multiplication of the principal sum by the interest rate (i.e. $P \times i = \$100,000 \times 10\%$ per annum), which is similar to the calculation of simple interest. However, the interest payment shown in Table 1.3 is, in fact, a compound interest calculation, with the *new balances* (i.e. column 3) remain unchanged at $100,000, the same as the principal, over the whole period of loan recovery, that is, five years. In such a case, the interest is actually charged annually to the *new balance* (i.e. by compound interest calculation), *as if* it is charged to the principal sum (i.e. by simple interest calculation).

Method 4

In the light of Method 3, we can think of another alternative in recovering the loan. We can separate the annual installment into two components:
(1) $P \times i$ = principal sum $\times$ i percent per annum (as if it is a simple interest calculation), and
(2) a sinking fund payment (see Section 3.4) of $P \times (ussff)^{n,i}$ for final redemption of the principal borrowed.

Table 1.4 illustrates this clearly:

Table 1.4 Single redempting payment and sinking funds.

	(1)	(2)	(3)	(4)	(5)
End of year	Principal borrowed	Principal amortization	Annual sinking fund for redemption of $100,000	Interest (same as Col 4 in Table 1.3)	Annual instalment (Col 3 + Col 4)
0	100,000				
1		0	16,379	10,000	26,379
2		0	16,379	10,000	26,379
3		0	16,379	10,000	26,379
4		0	16,379	10,000	26,379
5		100,000	16,379	10,000	26,379

(*Note*: Sinking fund $= \$100,000 \times (ussff)^{n=5, i=10\%}$
$= \$100,000 \times (0.16379) = \$16,379)$

In this method, the annual instalment is uniform.

Method 5

Lastly, we have the simplest method of calculating the uniform payment for recovering the loan:
Annual instalment $= 100,000 \times (uscrf)^{n=5, i=10\%}$
$= 100,000 \times (0.26379)$
$= 26,379$

Of course, the results obtained by Methods 4 and 5 are the same although different approaches have been used. By comparing the two methods, it can be observed that:

$100,000 \times (ussff)^{n,i} + 100,000 \times i = 100,000 \times (uscrf)^{n,i}$
i.e. $P \times (ussff)^{n,i} + P \times i = P \times (uscrf)^{n,i}$
or $(ussff)^{n,i} + i = (uscrf)^{n,i}$

So let us go back to Examples 1.3 and 1.4. By now the reader should not feel mystified about the coincidence. $P \times i$ in that case is ($\$125,000 \times 8\%$) and is equal to $\$10,000$. Hence, the sinking fund of $\$21,306$ (Example 1.3) added to $P \times i$, which is $\$10,000$, will naturally be equal to $\$31,306$ (Example 1.4).

Therefore, one can calculate the value of the annual instalment in Example 1.4 by either one of the following methods:

(1) Annua instalment $= 125,000 \times (\text{uscrf})^{n=5, i=8\%}$
$= 125,000 \times (0.25045)$
$= \$31,306$

or

(2) (a) Annual interest paid for the loan of $\$125,000$
$= 125,000 \times 8\% =$ $\$10,000$
(b) Annual sinking fund contributing to
a sum of $\$125,000$ in 5 years
$= 125,000 \times (\text{ussff})^{n=5, i=8\%}$
$= 125,000 \times (0.17045) =$ $\underline{\$21,306}$
Total annual instalment $\$31,306$

We can obtain the relationship that $(\text{ussff})^{n,i} + i = (\text{uscrf})^{n,i}$ purely by algebra as well:

$$(\text{ussff})^{n,i} + i = \frac{i}{(1+i)^n - 1} + i$$

$$= \frac{i + i(1+i)^n - i}{(1+i)^n - 1}$$

$$= \frac{i(1+i)^n}{(1+i)^n - 1} = (\text{uscrf})^{n,i}$$

Let us look at a further example.

Example 1.6

A man has borrowed $\$100,000$ from a bank which charges him 12% interest per annum. He has to recover the loan in 12 months.
(a) How much should he pay at the end of each month to the bank (assuming uniform payment)?
(b) If he wants to make an early redemption (i.e. pay all the money which he owes the bank) at the end of month 4, how much should he pay?
(c) If the bank negotiates with him not to redeem but to reduce the interest rate from 12% p.a. to 10% p.a., and if he agrees to the bank's

suggestion, what uniform amount will he pay at the end of each month for the remaining 8 months?

Solution 1.6

(a) Monthly payment = $100,000 \times (uscrf)^{n=12, i=1\%}$
$$= 100,000 \times 0.08885$$
$$= \$8,885$$

(b)

Month	Principal unpaid	Monthly payment	Interest	Principal paid	Remaining principal
1	100,000	8,885	$100,000 \times 1\%$ = 1,000	$8,885 - 1,000$ = 7,885	$100,000 - 7,885$ = 92,115
2	92,115	8,885	$92,115 \times 1\%$ = 921	$8,885 - 921$ = 7,964	$92,115 - 7,964$ = 84,151
3	84,151	8,885	$84,151 \times 1\%$ = 842	$8,885 - 842$ = 8,043	$84,151 - 8,043$ = 76,108
4	76,108	8,885	$76,108 \times 1\%$ = 761	$8,885 - 761$ = 8,124	$76,108 - 8,124$ = 67,984

Therefore, if the customer wants to redeem his loan at the end of month 4, he has to pay $8,885 plus $67,984. The latter is the remaining unpaid principal.

There is a short cut to calculate the amount $67,984 as follows:
The remaining unpaid principal = $8,885 \times (uspwf)^{n=12-4, i=1\%}$
$$= 8,885 \times 7.6517$$
$$= \$67,984$$

(c) The amount paid each month from years 5 to 12
$$= 67,984 \times (uscrf)^{n=8, i=10/12\%}$$
$$= 67,894 \times 0.12973 = 8,808$$

1.6 Mathematical Proof for the Same NPWs Obtained from Methods 1, 2 and 3 in Section 1.5

We have seen in Section 1.5 that no matter which method we use to pay back the loan, the present worths of the payments are the same. The following shows a rigorous mathematical proof for the phenomenon.

Let P = principal borrowed,

A = principal amortization in year i,

$R = 1 + i$ (i = borrowing interest rate, % p.a.), and

n = number of years.

Then, from Tables 1.1, 1.2 and 1.3, we can derive that:

PW of the first year instalment = $\dfrac{A_1 + PR - P}{R}$

PW of the second year instalment = $\dfrac{A_2 + (P - A_1)R - (P - A_1)}{R^2}$

PW of the third year instalment = $\dfrac{A_3 + (P - A_1 - A_2)R - (P - A_1 - A_2)}{R^3}$

.

.

.

PW of the nth year instalment

$= \dfrac{A_n + (P - A_1 - ... - A_{n-1})R - (P - A_1 - ... - A_{n-1})}{R^n}$

Now we use mathematical induction to prove that:

$$\dfrac{A_1 + PR - P}{R} + \dfrac{A_2 + (P - A_1)R - (P - A_1)}{R^2} + \dfrac{A_3 + (P - A_1 - A_2)R - (P - A_1 - A_2)}{R^3}$$

$$+ ... + \dfrac{A_n + (P - A_1 - ... - A_{n-1})R - (P - A_1 - ... - A_{n-1})}{R^n}$$

$$= \dfrac{(A_1 + A_2 + ... + A_n) + PR^n - P}{R^n}$$

Firstly, we must prove that the above mathematical expression is true when $n = 2$.

When $n = 2$,

$$\text{LHS} = \dfrac{A_1 + PR - P}{R} + \dfrac{A_2 + (P - A_1)R - (P - A_1)}{R^2}$$

$$= \dfrac{A_1 R + PR^2 - PR + A_2 + PR - A_1 R - P + A_1}{R^2}$$

$$= \dfrac{(A_1 + A_2) + PR^2 - P}{R^2} = \text{RHS}$$

So, the mathematical expression is true when $n = 2$.

Next, we must also prove that if the mathematical expression is true when $n = k$, it will also be true when $n = k + 1$.

When $n = k + 1$,

LHS

$$= \frac{A_1 + PR - P}{R} + \frac{A_2 + (P - A_1)R - (P - A_1)}{R^2}$$

$$+ \frac{A_3 + (P - A_1 - A_2)R - (P - A_1 - A_2)}{R^3} + ...$$

$$+ \frac{A_k + (P - A_1 - ... - A_{k-1})R - (P - A_1 - ... - A_{k-1})}{R^k}$$

$$+ \frac{A_{k+1} + (P - A_1 - ... - A_k)R - (P - A_1 - ... - A_k)}{R^{k+1}}$$

$$= \frac{(A_1 + A_2 + ... + A_k) + PR^k - P}{R^k}$$

$$+ \frac{A_{k+1} + (P - A_1 - ... - A_k)R - (P - A_1 - ... - A_k)}{R^{k+1}}, \qquad \text{as it is true for } n = k$$

$$= \frac{1}{R^{k+1}}(A_1 R + A_2 R + ... + A_k R + PR^{k+1} - PR + A_{k+1} + PR - A_1 R - A_2 R - ...$$

$$- A_k R - P + A_1 + ... + A_k)$$

$$= \frac{(A_1 + A_2 + ... + A_{k+1}) + PR^{k+1} - P}{R^{k+1}} = \text{RHS}$$

Therefore, the mathematical expression is true.

Hence, the total PWs of all the instalments

$$= \frac{(A_1 + A_2 + ... + A_n) + PR^n - P}{R^n}$$

$$= \frac{P + PR^n - P}{R^n}, \qquad \text{as } P = A_1 + A_2 + ... + A_n$$

$$= P$$

The proof is thus completed.

1.7 Problems

1. Explain the following:
    (a) apparent rate of growth in salary;
    (b) real rate of growth in salary.
    Is the interest rate of a bank apparent, or is it real?

2. (a) A bank pays 12% interest per annum, but interest payment is on a half yearly basis. If $1,000 is deposited on 1 January, providing no withdrawal is made, how much will be in the account on:
        (i)   30 June of the same year?
        (ii) 31 December of the same year?
        (*Hint*: 1 period = half a year, interest = 6% per period)
    (b) The bank still pays 12% interest per annum, but interest payment is on a quarterly basis. How much will be in the account on 31 December of the same year?
    (c) If the bank keeps paying 12% interest per annum, how much will be in the account on 31 December if it pays interest
        (i)   on monthly basis?
        (ii) on daily basis?
    (d) If the bank offers to pay interest (at 12% per annum) as often as the customer chooses, what will be the maximum amount in the account at the end of the year?

        (*Hint*: take the limit of $1000 \times (1 + \dfrac{0.12}{n})^n$ for $n \to \infty$. Remember

        that $\lim\limits_{n \to \infty} (1 + \dfrac{x}{n})^n = e^x$)

3. A company has borrowed $1,000,000 from a bank which charges the former 14% interest per annum. The loan has to be recovered in 5 years compounded annually.
    (a) How much should the company pay at the end of each year to the bank (assuming uniform payment)?
    (b) The bank changes the interest rate to 13% p.a. at the beginning of the third year.
        (i)   What will the amount of the company's last payment (i.e. payment at the end of year 5) if it keeps on paying the bank the same amount as calculated in (a) above at the end of years 3 and 4?
        (ii) What will be the company's repayment schedule if it chooses to pay back the bank in the form of uniform payments at the end of years 3, 4 and 5?

2. Economic Appraisal of Projects

So far, i has been treated as the interest rate or has sometimes been considered as the rate of return of an investment. Generally, i is called the *discount
rate* when it is used in the *equivalence calculation,* a term usually referred to
as the *equivalent annual cost* and the *present worth* methods in the economic
appraisal of projects.

2.1 Equivalent Annual Cost Method

Look at Fig. 1.5 and equation 1.12 in Chapter 1 again. We can interpret A as
the equivalent annual cost of the investment P. For instance, if a man purchases a colour television set at $5,000, the useful life of it is, say, five
years, and by assuming that the television set will be of zero value after five
years, the annual cost to the man of owning it will be $1,000 per year if the
discount rate i is taken as zero. The television set depreciates by $1,000 per
year to zero value in five years. However, if the time value of money is
taken into consideration, that is, if i equals a certain value, say, 10%, the
equivalent annual cost of owning the television set should then be calculated
as follows:

A = equivalent annual cost of owning the television set
   $= 5,000 \times (\text{uscrf})^{n=5, i=10\%}$
   $= 5,000 \times (0.26379)$
   $= \$1,319 \text{ p.a.}$

It should be noted that the equivalent annual cost of $1,319 is greater
than $1,000, simply because the time value of money has been accounted for
in the former figure but not in the latter one. It could be said that the initial
investment of $5,000 depreciates, in an economic sense, to zero value in a
period of five years. Repeating this important point again, the calculation of
the equivalent annual cost, which equals $1,319, has taken into account the
effect of depreciation of the asset. The reader should take special note of it
because double counting of depreciation in the financial analysis must be

avoided. Further explanation and examples will be given in Chapters 3, 6 and 7. Now let us look at the following diagrammatical illustrations.

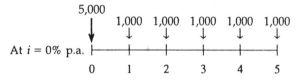

(The asset depreciates at $1,000 per year)

Fig. 2.1 Depreciation of asset at zero discount rate.

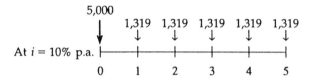

(The asset depreciates, including an interest
of 10% p.a., at $1,319 per year)

Fig. 2.2 Depreciation of asset at 10% discount rate.

It can be observed that the interest payable is $319 per annum (i.e. $1,319 - $1,000). Mathematically, this interest on finance can be calculated by

$$P \times (\text{uscrf})^{n,i} - \frac{P}{n}$$

Therefore, the equivalent annual cost can in fact be separated into two parts:

(a)   Annual depreciation of investment $= \dfrac{\$5,000}{5} = \$1,000$ p.a.

and

(b)   Interest on investment

$\qquad = \$5,000 \times (\text{uscrf})^{n=5, i=10\%} - \dfrac{\$5,000}{5}$

$\qquad = \$1,319 - \$1,000 \qquad\qquad\qquad = \underline{\$319 \text{ p.a.}}$

∴   Equivalent annual cost $\qquad\qquad = \$1,319$ p.a.

The following example will illustrate how the equivalent annual cost can be applied in the economic appraisal of projects.

Example 2.1

The construction cost of a sewerage system is estimated to be $30,000,000. The annual operation, maintenance and repair (i.e. OMR) cost will be $1,000,000 per year. The annual income (i.e. benefit) from the collection of sanitation fees from the users will be $3,500,000. Taking a time horizon of 30 years and a discount rate of 5%, determine if the project is financially viable.

Solution 2.1

Annual benefit = $3,500,000
Annual OMR cost = $1,000,000
Equivalent annual cost of construction
    $= 30,000,000 \times (\text{uscrf})^{n=30, i=5\%}$
    $= 30,000,000 \times (0.06505) =$ $1,951,500 $2,951,500
Net annual benefit (NAB) = $548,500

There is a positive *net annual benefit* (i.e. *total annual benefits – total annual costs*) and therefore the project is viable.

2.2 Present Worth Method

The meaning of present worth has been explained in Section 4 of Chapter 1. The following is an example illustrating the application of present worth in the economic appraisal of projects.

Example 2.2

Repeat doing Example 2.1 by the present worth method.

Solution 2.2

Present worth of benefits in 30 years
    $= 3,500,000 \times (\text{uspwf})^{n=30, i=5\%}$
    $= 3,500,000 \times (15.3724) =$ $53,803,400
Present worth of construction cost = $30,000,000
Present worth of OMR cost
    $= 1,000,000 \times (\text{uspwf})^{n=30, i=5\%}$
    $= 1,000,000 \times (15.3724) =$ $15,372,400 $45,372,400
Net present worth (NPW) = $ 8,431,000

The positive *net present worth* (i.e. *present worth of total benefits – present worth of total costs*) indicated that the project is viable.

It should be noted that there exists a relation between Solution 2.1 and Solution 2.2:

$$\$8,431,000 \times (\text{uscrf})^{n=30, i=5\%} = \$548,500$$

2.3 Benefit-Cost Ratio (B/C Ratio)

The B/C ratio is defined as follows:

(a)   B/C ratio $= \dfrac{\text{Equivalent annual total benefits}}{\text{Equivalent annual total costs}}$ or

(b)   B/C ratio $= \dfrac{\text{Present worth of total benefits}}{\text{Present worth of total costs}}$

Both of the above definitions give the same answers. Take Example 2.1 (the sewerage project) as an example:

$$\text{B/C ratio} = \frac{3,500,000}{2,951,500} = 1.186 \qquad\qquad \text{(by definition (a))}$$

$$\text{B/C ratio} = \frac{53,803,400}{45,372,400} = 1.186 \qquad\qquad \text{(by definition (b))}$$

If the B/C ratio is greater than 1, the project is worthwhile, and vice versa. A B/C ratio of exactly 1 means that the project will break-even. A project having a positive net annual benefit or a positive net present worth must have a B/C ratio greater than 1. Similarly, a project having a negative net annual benefit or a negative net present worth will have a B/C ratio less than 1.

Before going further, let us see a few more complicated examples of project appraisal by the methods of present worth and equivalent annual cost.

Example 2.3

Consider the relative costs of a timber pedestrian bridge and a steel one: their initial capital costs, annual OMR costs and useful lives are given below:

	Timber bridge	Steel bridge
Initial capital	$500,000	$700,000
Annual OMR cost	$30,000	$5000
Life	15 years	30 years

Find the alternative of the least overall costs (use $i = 8\%$).

Solution 2.3

(A) Firstly, let us use the *present worth method* to compare the two alternatives. In order to have a fair comparison, we must set the two alternatives to have the same benefits. In order that they have the same benefits, we must assume that both alternatives can be used for the same number of years, 30 in this case. The timber bridge must be renewed after the first 15 years.

		Timber bridge *(Life 15 years)*	Steel bridge *(Life 30 years)*
(a)	Initial capital	**$500,000**	**$700,000**
(b)	Present worth of OMRcosts over 30 years	$30,000 \times (\text{uspwf})^{n=30,i=8\%}$ $= 30,000 \times (11.2577)$ $= $ **$337,731**	$5,000 \times (\text{uspwf})^{n=30,i=8\%}$ $= 5,000 \times (11.2577)$ $= $ **$56,288**
(c)	Present worth of renewal	$500,000 \times (\text{pwf})^{n=15,i=8\%}$ $= 500,000 \times (0.31524)$ $= $ **$157,620**	**0**
(d)	Present worth of total costs	**$995,351**	**$756,288**

(The two figures bear a ratio of 1.316)

The steel bridge thus has the least overall costs.

Note: As we must compare a 30-year period for both alternatives, and because the life of the timber bridge is only 15 years, a new one, for comparison purposes, will have to be built at the end of year 15 and hence a capital of $500,000 will have to be laid out at that time, the present worth of which is $157,620, calculated as shown in item (c) above. Readers are once more reminded that an inflation-free world has been assumed. Therefore, the construction cost of the timber bridge at that time will still be $500,000.

(B) Secondly, we use the equivalent annual cost method to compare the alternatives.

		Timber bridge *(Life 15 years)*	Steel bridge *(Life 30 years)*
(a)	Equivalent annual cost of initial capital	$500,000 \times (\text{uscrf})^{n=15,i=8\%}$ $= 500,000 \times (0.11682)$ $= $ **$58,410**	$700,000 \times (\text{uscrf})^{n=30,i=8\%}$ $= 700,000 \times (0.08882)$ $= $ **$62,174**
(b)	Annual OMR cost	**$30,000**	**$5,000**
(c)	Total equivalent annual costs	**$88,410**	**$67,174**

(The two figures also bear a ratio of 1.316)

The reader may puzzle why the life periods of the timber and steel bridges used in the equivalent annual cost calculation are 15 and 30 years respectively, while the life periods of the bridges in the present worth method is 30 years for both.

The explanation is that although the time horizons used in the equivalent annual cost method appear to be different, they are in fact the same because we have already compared the bridges using a 30 year time horizon. The equivalent annual cost from years 1 to 15 is $88,410 and the same figure applies to years 16 to 30, since we have assumed that there is no inflation. This means, of course, that the equivalent annual cost from years 1 to 30 is $88,410.

Again, consistent with the result obtained by the present worth method, the steel bridge has the lowest overall cost.

Observe that the following relations exist between the solutions in Methods (A) and (B):

(i) $\$995,351 \times (uscrf)^{n=30, i=8\%} = \$88,410$

(ii) $\$756,288 \times (uscrf)^{n=30, i=8\%} = \$67,174$

The readers should try to appreciate the underlying principle behind these two relations.

Example 2.4

Repeat doing Example 2.3 if the life of timber bridge is changed to 20 years.

Solution 2.4

(A) Present worth method (compare 60 years this time):

		Timber bridge (Life 20 years)	Steel bridge (Life 30 years)
(a)	Initial capital	**$500,000**	**$700,000**
(b)	Present worth of OMR costs over 60 years	$30,000 \times (uspwf)^{n=60, i=8\%}$ $= 30,000 \times (12.3765)$ $= $ **$371,295**	$5,000 \times (uspwf)^{n=60, i=8\%}$ $= 5,000 \times (12.3765)$ $= $ **$61,882**
(c)	Present worth of first renewal	$500,000 \times (pwf)^{n=20, i=8\%}$ $= 500,000 \times (0.21454)$ $= $ **$107,270**	$700,000 \times (pwf)^{n=30, i=8\%}$ $= 700,000 \times (0.09937)$ $= $ **$69,559**
(d)	Present worth of second renewal	$500,000 \times (pwf)^{n=40, i=8\%}$ $= 500,000 \times (0.04603)$ $= $ **$23,015**	**0**
(e)	Present worth of total costs	**$1,001,580**	**$831,441**

(B) Equivalent annual cost method:

	Timber bridge (Life 20 years)	Steel bridge (Life 30 years)
(a) Equivalent annual cost of initial capital	$500,000 \times (\text{uscrif})^{n=20, i=8\%}$ $= 500,000 \times (0.10185)$ $= \textbf{\$50,925}$	$700,000 \times (\text{uscrif})^{n=30, i=8\%}$ $= 700,000 \times (0.08882)$ $= \textbf{\$62,174}$
(b) Annual OMR cost	**$30,000**	**$5,000**
(c) Total equivalent annual costs	**$80,925**	**$67,174**

Observe that:

(i) $\$1,001,580 \times (\text{uscrf})^{n=60, i=8\%} = \$80,925$

(ii) $\$831,441 \times (\text{uscrf})^{n=60, i=8\%} = \$67,174$

Example 2.5

A new piece of equipment costs $100,000. The life of the equipment is estimated to be 15 years. During the first five years there will be no maintenance cost for it but thereafter the annual maintenance cost will be $20,000. The equipment is assumed to be useless at the end of its life. Compute the equivalent annual cost of owning it by taking $i = 10\%$.

Solution 2.5

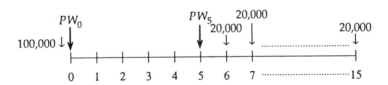

Fig. 2.3 Diagrammatic presentation of Example 2-5

Let PW_5 = the equivalent sum of money at the end of year 5 for the uniform series of payments of $20,000 per annum from year 6 to year 15.

Then, PW_5 = $20,000 \times (\text{uspwf})^{n=10, i=10\%} = 20,000 \times (6.1445)$
       = $122,890$

Let PW_0 = present worth of PW_5

Then, PW_0 = $PW_5 \times (\text{pwf})^{n=5, i=10\%} = 122,890 \times (0.62092)$
       = $76,305$

The total present worth = initial cost + PW_0
$$= 100,000 + 76,305$$
$$= \$176,305$$

The equivalent annual cost can be computed by spreading the total present worth into 15 yearly payments, taking into consideration the time value of money, and is equal to:

$176,305 \times (\text{uscrf})^{n=15,i=10\%} = \$176,305 \times (0.13147)$
= $ 23,179

2.4 Equivalent Annual Cost of An Asset with Salvage Value

The salvage value of an asset is its value after n years. If a new car costs $60,000, and if its cost drops to $10,000 five years later, the car is said to have a salvage value of $10,000 after five years. (Readers are reminded once more that the inflation-free assumption is still valid, and will conhnue to be valid until this issue is further discussed in Chapter 4). We usually use P to denote an asset's initial cost, and R its salvage value. Diagrammatically, P and R can be presented as follows:

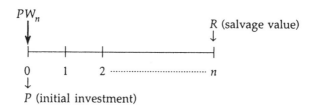

Fig. 2.4 Present worth of salvage value

Let PW_n = the present worth of the salvage value $R = R(\text{pwf})^{n,i}$
$\therefore$ Net present worth of investment = $P - PW_n$
$$= P - R(\text{pwf})^{n,i}$$

Let the equivalent annual cost of an asset with salvage value $R = A$.

$\therefore$ $A = [P - R(\text{pwf})^{n,i}] \times (\text{uscrf})^{n,i}$ (2.5)

Example 2.6

A car costs $60,000 when it is new. After five years it will be sold at a price of $10,000. What is the equivalent annual cost A if the discount rate is taken as 10%?

Solution 2.6

$P = \$60,000$
$R = \$10,000$
$n = 5$
$\therefore \quad A = [60,000 - 10,000(\text{pwf})^{n=5,i=10\%}](\text{uscrf})^{n=5,i=10\%}$
$\quad\quad = [60,000 - 10,000 \times (0.62092)] \times (0.26379)$
$\quad\quad = (60,000 - 6,209) \times (0.26379)$
$\quad\quad = \$14,190$

Equation (2.5) can be written mathematically as:

$$A = \left[P - \frac{R}{(1+i)^n}\right]\left[\frac{i(1+i)^n}{(1+i)^n - 1}\right]$$

$$= P\left[\frac{i(1+i)^n}{(1+i)^n - 1}\right] - R\left[\frac{i}{(1+i)^n - 1}\right]$$

$$= P\left[\frac{i(1+i)^n}{(1+i)^n - 1}\right] - R\left[\frac{i(1+i)^n}{(1+i)^n - 1}\right] - R\left[\frac{i}{(1+i)^n - 1}\right] + R\left[\frac{i(1+i)^n}{(1+i)^n - 1}\right]$$

$$= (P - R)\left[\frac{i(1+i)^n}{(1+i)^n - 1}\right] + R\left[\frac{i(1+i)^n - i}{(1+i)^n - 1}\right]$$

$$= (P - R)\left[\frac{i(1+i)^n}{(1+i)^n - 1}\right] + R \times i\left[\frac{(1+i)^n - 1}{(1+i)^n - 1}\right]$$

$$= (P - R) \times (\text{uscrf})^{n,i} + R \times i$$

Therefore equation (2.5) can be written as:

$$A = (P - R) \times (\text{uscrf})^{n,i} + R \times i \tag{2.6}$$

Example 2.7

Repeat doing Example 2.6 by using equation (2.6).

Solution 2.7

$P = \$60,000$
$R = \$10,000$
$n = 5$

$A = (60,000 - 10,000)(\text{uscrf})^{n=5,i=10\%} + 10,000 \times 10\%$

$$= 50,000 \times (0.26379) + 1,000 = 13,190 + 1,000$$
$$= \$14,190$$

Equations 2.6 and Solution 2.7 can be interpreted as follows:
The investment \$60,000 can be considered as consisting of two different parts:

(i)   \$50,000 (i.e. \$60,000 – \$10,000), which will depreciate to zero value, taking into account the time value of money, on an annual basis, calculated to be \$13,190 per annum, and;

(ii)   \$10,000, the salvage value, which is in effect loaned to the investment for the length of its life, thus needed to be charged at an interest of \$1,000 (i.e. \$10,000 × 10%) annually.

Example 2.8

A manager wanted to purchase a new personal computer (PC) for his company. He had been approached by two agents of different PC manufacturers offering their newest models. After detailed investigation he obtained the following estimates:

	PC-model A	PC-model B
Cost of PC	\$20,000	\$15,000
Annual maintenance cost	\$1,000 p.a.	\$1,800 p.a.
Salvage value	\$2,500	\$1,500
Life	5 years	5 years

Assuming $i = 12\%$, determine for the manager which model of PC he should purchase.

Solution 2.8

Let us compare the equivalent annual costs of the two models:

		PC-model A	PC-model B
(a)	Equivalent annual cost of capital	$(20,000 - 2,500)\times$ $(\text{uscrf})^{n=5, i=12\%}$ $+ 2,500 \times 12\%$ $= 17,500 \times (0.27740) + 300$ $= \mathbf{\$5,155}$	$(15,000 - 1,500)\times$ $(\text{uscrf})^{n=5, i=12\%}$ $+ 1,500 \times 12\%$ $= 13,500 \times (0.27740) + 180$ $= \mathbf{\$3,925}$
(b)	Annual maintenance cost	**\$1,000**	**\$1,800**
(c)	Total equivalent annual costs	**\$6,155**	**\$5,725**

Model B should be purchased as it has a lower total equivalent annual costs.

The comparison can also be done by the present worth method:

		PC-model A	PC-model B
(a)	Capital	**$20,000**	**$15,000**
(b)	Present worth of annual maintenance	$1,000 \times (\text{uspwf})^{n=5, i=12\%}$ $= 1,000 \times (3.6047)$ $=$ **$3,605**	$1,800 \times (\text{uspwf})^{n=5, i=12\%}$ $= 1,800 \times (3.6047)$ $=$ **$6,489**
(c)	*Less:* present worth of salvage	$-2,500 \times (\text{pwf})^{n=5, i=12\%}$ $= -2,500 \times (0.56742)$ $=$ **−$1,419**	$-1,500 \times (\text{pwf})^{n=5, i=12\%}$ $= -1,500 \times (0.56742)$ $=$ **−$851**
(d)	Present worth of total costs	**$22,186**	**$20,638**

The same conclusion can be drawn as model B has a lower present worth of total costs.

2.5 Problems

1. A company can hire a machine for an all-inclusive rate of $125 per hour and on average makes use of such a machine for 1600 hours per year. The company is considering purchasing a machine as an alternative to hire and obtain the information given below:

   Cost of machine = $320,000
   Salvage value after 5 years = $120,000
   Annual insurance premiums = $3,000
   Annual tax = $1,800
   Fuel cost per hour = $50
   Oil and grease = 10% of fuel
   Annual maintenance = $15,000
   Annual cost of capital = 18%

   Determine whether the company should purchase a new machine or continue to hire.

2. There are two alternatives for constructing a pedestrian bridge. Both serve the purpose of allowing people to cross a busy street but different life span and patterns of cash flow are associated with each as follows:

	Alternative 1	Alternative 2
Initial cost	$900,000	$1,300,000
OMR cost	$80,000 p.a.	$20,000 p.a.
Life	10 years	15 years

Assuming the discount rate to be 16% per annum, choose the better alternative by
(a) the equivalent annual cost method;
(b) the present worth method.

3. A section of roadway pavement costs $50,000 a year to maintain. What immediate expenditure for a replacement for the existing pavement is justifiable if the new pavement requires no maintenance in the first five years, $20,000 per year for the next 10 years, and $50,000 per year thereafter (assume money to cost 10% per annum)?

3. Discount Cash Flow Method

3.1 The Internal Rate of Return (IRR)

In Chapter 2, the methods described for project appraisal were based on a predetermined discount rate i. With a predetermined i for calculating the net present worth or the net annual benefit, the result can either be positive or negative (see Examples 2.1 and 2.2 of Chapter 2). If it is positive, the project is considered viable, and vice versa. However, we might sometimes obtain, by luck, a *zero* result of net present worth (or net annual benefit) with the use of a predetermined i. In such a case, the project is considered breaking-even since its present worth of total benefits equals its present worth of total costs (or the total annual benefits equal the total annual costs). The discount rate i, in this case, represents exactly the rate of return on the investment over its life, and is called IRR *(internal rate of return)*. Some people like to call it the *yield rate* or *solution rate.* Hence, IRR can be defined as the discount rate i that the net present worth of a project is zero if such i is used in the equivalence calculation.

In this chapter, the reader will see a full description of the discount cash flow (DCF) method which is a method to determine the IRR of an investment, with costs and benefits known (or estimated) over the time span of the investment. Readers should note that it is not necessary for the DCF method to use a predetermined i.

3.2 Mathematical Presentation of IRR

Let C_k = total cash outflow (i.e. expenditure or cost) in year k,
      B_k = total cash inflow (i.e. income or benefit) in year k,
    NCF_k = net cash flow in year k.
By definition:

$$NCF_k = B_k - C_k \qquad\qquad (3.1)$$

The cash flows can be tabulated as in Table 3.1:

Table 3.1 A typical cash flow table

End of Year	(1) Cash out	(2) Cash in	(3) Net cash flow (Col 2 – Col 1)
0	C_0	B_0	NCF_0
1	C_1	B_1	NCF_1
2	C_2	B_2	NCF_2
.	.	.	.
.	.	.	.
.	.	.	.
k	C_k	B_k	NCF_k
.	.	.	.
.	.	.	.
.	.	.	.
n	C_n	B_n	NCF_n

The *net present worth* (NPW) can be obtained by:

$$NPW = \sum_{k=0}^{n} \frac{B_k}{(1+i)^k} - \sum_{k=0}^{n} \frac{C_k}{(1+i)^k}$$

or $$NPW = \sum_{k=0}^{n} \frac{B_k - C_k}{(1+i)^k} \tag{3.2}$$

By substituting equation (3.1) into equation (3.2), the following equation is obtained:

$$NPW = \sum_{k=0}^{n} \frac{NCF_k}{(1+i)^k} \tag{3.3}$$

or $$NPW = \frac{NCF_0}{1} + \frac{NCF_1}{1+i} + \frac{NCF_2}{(1+i)^2} + \cdots + \frac{NCF_n}{(1+i)^n} \tag{3.3a}$$

If i = IRR (i.e. NPW = 0), then

$$\frac{NCF_0}{1} + \frac{NCF_1}{1+i} + \frac{NCF_2}{(1+i)^2} + \cdots + \frac{NCF_n}{(1+i)^n} = 0 \tag{3.4}$$

or $$\sum_{k=0}^{n} \frac{NCF_k}{(1+i)^k} = 0 \tag{3.4a}$$

So, IRR can be calculated by solving equation (3.4). It is, however, not easy to solve such a complicated equation algebraically. The following section will describe a simpler method, but less accurate of course, for the calculation of IRR. The result so obtained would be good enough for practical use.

3.3 Calculation of IRR by Interpolation

The best way to illustrate the calculation procedures is to use an example.

Example 3.1

Find the IRR of an investment of $10,000 whose receipts in the next 3 years are $4,000, $4,500 and $5,000 respectively.

Solution 3.1

The calculation of IRR is best performed in a tabulated manner as shown in Table 3.2.

Table 3.2 Calculation of IRR

End of year	(1) Cash out	(2) Cash in	(3) NCF (2) − (1)	(4) $(pwf)^{10\%}$	(5) $(DCF)^{10\%}$ (3) × (4)	(6) $(pwf)^{20\%}$	(7) $(DCF)^{20\%}$ (3) × (6)
0	10,000		−10,000	1	−10,000	1	−10,000
1		4,000	4,000	090909	3,636	083333	3,333
2		4,500	4,500	082644	3,719	069444	3,125
3		5,000	5,000	075131	3,757	057870	2,894
				$(NPW)^{10\%} = 1,112$		$(NPW)^{20\%} = -648$	

Legend: Col 1: Data given.
  Col 2: Data given.
  Col 3: NCF = Col 2 − Col 1 (as defined in Section 3.2)
  Col 4: the 10% pwf is entered arbitrarily. The values of $(pwf)^{n,10\%}$ can be copied directly from the compound interest table in Appendix 1.
  Col 5: $(DCF)^{10\%}$ is in fact the present worth of NCF in any year at a 10% discount rate. The sum of the whole column of DCFs is the NPW.
  Col 6: the 20% pwf is entered arbitrarily. The values of $(pwf)^{n,20\%}$ can be copied directly from the compound interest table in Appendix 1.
  Col 7: $(DCF)20\%$ is in fact the present worth of NCF in any year at a 20% discount rate. The sum of the whole column of DCFs is the NPW.

If pwf = 10%, NPW = 1,112; if pwf = 20%, NPW = –648; and there exists an *i* where 10% < *i* < 20% such that the NPW = 0 if such *i*% is used in the above calculation.

This *i*, or more exactly the IRR, can be found approximately by interpolation as shown in Fig. 3.1.

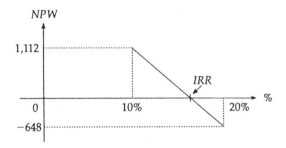

Fig. 3.1 Obtaining IRR by interpolation

$$\text{IRR} = 10\% + \left(\frac{1{,}112}{1{,}112 + 648} \right)(20 - 10)\% = 10\% + 0.63 \times 10\% = 16.3\%$$

Note 1:   Strictly speaking, the straight line drawn in Fig. 3.1 is wrong as the relation of NPW and *i* is not linear (see equation (3.4)). The interpolated IRR is an approximate solution only. The readers can try to reduce the difference of the two arbitrary discount rates (i.e. 10% and 20% as used in the example) to, say, 15% and 18% and do the whole exercise again. An improved solution can be obtained. Computer programs are available for performing such iterations for finding IRR (see Appendix 3).

Note 2:   It can be observed that the values of the NPW are high (usually positive) for small values of *i* and are low (usually negative) for large values of *i*. If a curve of NPW versus *i* is plotted, it will appear in a shape as shown in Fig. 3.2, which looks like the shape of Fig. 3.1.

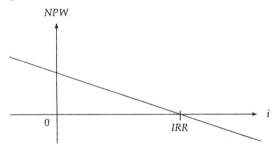

Fig. 3.2 Shape of NPW vs. *i* graph

Note 3: The curve in Fig. 3.2 *is not* a straight line. It is drawn straight only for convenience's sake to show the general form of relation between NPW and *i*.

Note 4: The curve shown in Fig. 3.2 is true for the cases when the NCFs of the project life are of the type as shown in Table 3.3. Such a curve shape does not apply if the NCFs of the project life are of the type as shown in Table 3.4. This point will be further discussed in Sections 3.5, 3.6 and 3.7.

<table>
<tr><td colspan="2">Table 3.3 Initial negative NCF and subsequent positive NCFs</td></tr>
<tr><th>End of year</th><th>NCF</th></tr>
<tr><td>0</td><td>Negative</td></tr>
<tr><td>1</td><td>Positive</td></tr>
<tr><td>2</td><td>Positive</td></tr>
<tr><td>3</td><td>Positive</td></tr>
<tr><td>4</td><td>Positive</td></tr>
<tr><td>5</td><td>Positive</td></tr>
<tr><td>6</td><td>Positive</td></tr>
<tr><td>7</td><td>Positive</td></tr>
<tr><td>.</td><td>.</td></tr>
<tr><td>.</td><td>.</td></tr>
<tr><td>.</td><td>.</td></tr>
<tr><td>n</td><td>Positive</td></tr>
</table>

Table 3.3 Initial negative NCF and subsequent positive NCFs

End of year	NCF
0	Negative
1	Positive
2	Positive
3	Positive
4	Positive
5	Positive
6	Positive
7	Positive
.	.
.	.
.	.
n	Positive

Table 3.4 Positive and negative NCFs fluctuating within project life

End of year	NCF
0	Negative
1	Positive
2	Positive
3	Negative
4	Positive
5	Positive
6	Negative
7	Positive
.	.
.	.
.	.
n	Positive

Example 3.2

A man has the opportunity of investing $9,000,000 in either Business A or Business B whose estimated incomes in the next 10 years are shown in Tables 3.5 and 3.6 respectively.

Determine for the investor which business he shoud invest in so as to obtain the maximum benefit.

Solution 3.2

Another advantage of tabulating the cash flow is that it would enable different expenditures or incomes in different years to be shown clearly and that the present worths of non-uniform annual NCFs could be evaluted in a systmatic manner. The use of $(uspwf)^{n,i}$ in calculating present worths, as described previously, could only be applicable to uniform annual payments, and is therefore less flexible.

Table 3.5 Cash flows of Business A

End of year	Cash out	Cash in
0	9,000,000	
1		500,000
2		800,000
3		1,200,000
4		1,500,000
5	200,000	2,000,000
6		2,000,000
7		4,200,000
8		5,000,000

Table 3.6 Cash flows of Busioess B

End of year	Cash out	Cash in
0	9,000,000	
1		2,500,000
2		2,300,000
3		2,000,000
4		1,500,000
5	300,000	1,500,000
6		1,000,000
7	200,000	1,000,000
8		800,000
9	200,000	800,000
10		600,000

Table 3.7 Calculation of IRR for Business A

End of year	(1) Cash out ($ \times 10^3$)	(2) Cash in ($ \times 10^3$)	(3) NCF (2) – (1)	(4) $(pwf)^{8\%}$	(5) $(DCF)^{8\%}$ (3) \times (4)	(6) $(pwf)^{16\%}$	(7) $(DCF)^{16\%}$ (3) \times (6)
0	9,000		−9,000	1.00000	−9,000	1.00000	−9,000
1		500	500	0.92592	463	0.86206	431
2		800	800	0.85733	686	0.74316	595
3		1,200	1,200	0.79383	953	0.64065	769
4		1,500	1,500	0.73502	1,103	0.55229	828
5	200	2,000	1,800	0.68058	1,225	0.47611	857
6		2,000	2,000	0.63016	1,260	0.41044	821
7		4,200	4,200	0.58349	2,451	0.35382	1,486
8		5,000	5,000	0.54026	2,701	0.30502	1,525
					$(NPW)^{8\%} = 1,842$		$(NPW)^{16\%} = -1,688$

(The discount rates of 8% and 16% in Table 3.5 are arbitrarily chosen.)

Firsstly, find the IRR of Business A
If pwf = 8%, the NPW = 1,842; and
if pwf = 16%, the NPW = −1,688.

The IRR can be found approximately by interpolation as shown in Fig. 3.3 below:

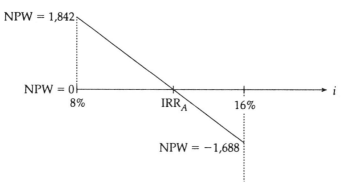

Fig. 3.3 Obtaining IRR by interpolation for Business B

$$IRR_A = 8\% + \left(\frac{1,842}{1,842 + 1,688} \right)(16 - 8)\% = 8\% + 0.522 \times 8\% = 12.2\%$$

Secondly, find the IRR of Business B.

Table 3.8 Calculation of IRR for business B

End of year	NCF	(pwf)$^{8\%}$	(DCF)$^{8\%}$	(pwf)$^{12\%}$	(DCF)$^{12\%}$
0	−9,000	1.00000	−9,000	1.00000.	−9,000
1	2,500	0.92592	2,315	0.89285	2,232
2	2,300	0.85733	1,972	0.79719	1,834
3	2,000	0.79383	1,588	0.71178	1,424
4	1,500	0.73502	1,103	0.63551	953
5	1,200	0.68058	817	0.56742	681
6	1,000	0.63016	630	0.50663	507
7	800	0.58349	467	0.45234	362
8	800	0.54026	432	0.40388	323
9	600	0.50024	300	0.36061	216
10	600	0.46319	278	0.32197	193
		(NPW)$^{8\%}$ = 902		(NPW)$^{12\%}$ = −275	

The IRR can be found approximately by interpolation as shown in Fig. 3.4:

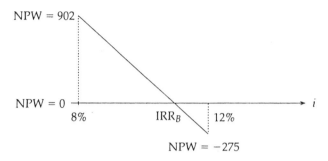

Fig. 3.4 Obtaining IRR by interpolation for Business B

$$IRR_B = 8\% + \left(\frac{902}{902 + 275}\right)(12 - 8)\% = 11\%$$

By comparing the two IRRs: $IRR_A = 12.2\%$ and $IRR_B = 11\%$, the conclusion is that the man should invest in Business A as it has a higher rate of return than Business B.

Note: In this example, we do not have to compare the two alternatives using the same number of years as we have done in Examples 2.3 and 2.4 in Chapter 2. In Examples 2.3 and 2.4, we used the same number of years because we wanted them to have a same datum for comparison — same benefits. In Example 3.2, however, we have already had a same datum — same capital costs (this can be easily seen if we look at their NCF columns in Tables 3.7 and 3.8). The readers are expected to have a right concept about this. This point will be further discussed in Section 4 of Chapter 5.

3.4 Underlying Principles of DCF Method

The DCF method is, similar to other methods previously discussed, based on the discount of future cash flows by taking account of the time value of money. The DCF method, like the equivalent annual cost method, also automatically allows the initial investment to depreciate over the life of the project (see Section 1 of Chapter 2). Since IRR is calculated by equation (3.4), the calculation is in fact based on the outstanding balance (or the undepreciated part) of the capital invested, having allowed for net incomes to offset against the investment. This point might be a little difficult for the reader to appreciate, but it could be made easier if they look back to Section 5 of Chapter 1. All the five examples illustrated in that section were of IRR = 10% and present worth (or NCF_0) = $100,000, where

$$-NCF_0 = 100,000 = \sum_{k=1}^{5} \frac{NCF_k}{(1+10\%)^k}$$

which is actually equation (3.4) or equation (3.4a) for $n = 5$ and $i = 10\%$. What the readers should do is to treat the loan, $100,000, as capital investment and the annual installments as annual incomes.

Take the example of Method 1 illustrated in Section 5 of Chapter 1. Readers can treat the problem as one whose NCFs are shown below in Table 3.9:

Table 3.9 Summary of cash flows of Table 1.1

End of year	NCF
0	−100,000
1	30,000
2	28,000
3	26,000
4	24,000
5	22,000

By the end of the first year the loss due to the cost of the capital, $100,000, amounts to $10,000 (at 10%). $10,000 therefore must be deducted from the first year's income, $30,000, to cover the loss. A net available sum of $20,000 (i.e. $30,000 − $10,000) is left to be offset against a part of the capital investment, leaving an outstanding balance (or the undepreciated part of the capital) of $80,000 (i.e. $100,000 − $20,000). It is then necessary to calculate the cost of the remaining capital, $80,000, at 10%, due to the end of the second year. The amounts to $8,000. Deducting this $8,000 from the income of the second year, $28,000, there is a net income of $20,000 (i.e. $28,000 − $8,000). This $20,000 is used again to payoff the remaining (or the undepreciated) capital debt, $80,000, leaving an outstanding capital debt of $60,000 (i.e. $80,000 − $20,000). Again, the loss due to the cost of the remaining capital, $60,000, due at the end of the third year at 10% is $6,000.

The net income in the third year is therefore $20,000 (i.e. $26,000 − $6,000). This net income, $20,000, is used to offset the remaining (or the undepreciated) investment debt, $60,000, and hence the remaining debt is $40,000 (i.e. $60,000 − $20,000). In the fourth year, the cost of capital amounts to $4,000, 10% of the remaining (or the undepreciated) capital debt.

Deducting it from $24,000, the income in the fourth year, gives a net income of $20,000 (i.e. $24,000 -$4,000). The remaining investment debt at the end of year 4 is therefore $20,000 (i.e. $40,000 – $20,000).

Finally, the cost of capital in the fifth year is calculated to be $2,000 (i.e. 10% of $20,000). The net income in Year 5 is therefore $20,000 (i.e. $22,000 – $2,000), which just clears the outstanding undepreciated investment debt, which is also exactly $20,000.

The DCF method thus takes account of depreciation automatically inasmuch as it allows for the capital investment to be offset against by theincomes over the life of the investment. Let us illustrate this point by the following example.

Example 3.3

A piece of equipment is purchased at a cost of $40,000. Its useful life is 5 years and the annual OMR cost is estimated to be $11,000 p.a. The manager of the company is thinking of hiring it out so that he has to estimate the minimum (i.e. at break-even condition) hire rate on a per day basis. Assuming the average number of days that the equipment could be for hire is 300 a year, estimate the minimum hire charge per day for the manager (take $i = 18\%$).

Solution 3.3

There are two methods for finding the solution.

Method 1
(Readers should refer to Section 1 of Chapter 2 for this method)

Annual depreciation (straight line) $= \dfrac{40,000}{5} =$ $8,000 p.a.

Annual interest on investment

$= 40,000 \times (\text{uscrf})^{n=5, i=18\%} - \dfrac{40,000}{5}$

$= 12,790 - 8,000 =$ $4,790 p.a.

Annual OMR costs $=$ $11,000 p.a.

Total annual costs $=$ $23,790 p.a.

$\therefore$ Minimum hire charge per day $= \dfrac{\$23,790}{300} = \$79.30$

Method 2

End of year	(1) Capital	(2) OMR	(3) Depre-ciation	(4) Total	(5) Annual hire charge	(6) (5) – (4)	(6) + Depre ciation
			(Cash out)		(Cash-in)		
0	40,000			40,000		–40,000	–40,000
1		11,000	8,000	19,000	x	$x - 19,000$	$x - 11,000$
2		11,000	8,000	19,000	x	$x - 19,000$	$x - 11,000$
3		11,000	8,000	19,000	x	$x - 19,000$	$x - 11,000$
4		11,000	8,000	19,000	x	$x - 19,000$	$x - 11,000$
5		11,000	8,000	19,000	x	$x - 19,000$	$x - 11,000$

As the DCF method has automatically allowed for depreciation, double counting must be avoided. To accomplish this, depreciation has to be added to column (6) so that:

$$40,000 = (x - 11,000)(\text{uspwf})^{n=5, i=18\%}$$

i.e. $40,000 = 3.1271x - 34,398$

$$x = \frac{40,000 + 34,398}{3.1271} = \$23,790 \text{ per year}$$

$$= \frac{23,790}{300} \text{ or } \$79.30 \text{ per day (the same answer is obtained)}$$

Example 3.4

A bank offers personal loan to a customer at a flat rate of 0.7% per month. On top of charging interest, the bank also requires from the customer a handling fee equal to 1% of the loan amount payable at the beginning of the redemption period. If the customer wishes to borrow $100,000 from the bank and redeem it in 9 months, what will be the equivalent nominal annual interest rate expressed in % p.a. that the bank is actually charging him?

Solution 3.4

Handling fee = $100,000 × 1% = $1,000
Effective loan = $100,000 + $1,000 = $101,000

Total interest = $101,000 × 0.7% × 9 = $6,363

∴   Monthly payment to bank by customer = $\dfrac{101,000 + 6,363}{9}$ = $11,929

The cash flow table is therefore as follows:

End of month	Cash out	Cash in
0	100,000	
1		11,929
2		11,929
3		11,929
4		11,929
5		11,929
6		11,929
7		11,929
8		11,929
9		11,929

The IRR of the above cash flow is 1.445% p.m.

∴   The equivalent nominal annual interest rate = 1.445% × 12 = 17.34% p.a. That is, the customer is actually paying an interest rate of 17.34% p.a. to the bank.

3.5 Multiple Root Problem

Equation (3.4) in Section 2, from which the IRRs are calculated, is a polynomial equation. It is possible for a polynomial equation to have, besides roots of imaginary numbers, more than one root of real numbers. Among these real roots, some may be negative and some positive. Apparently, the negative roots can be ignored as they represent negative IRRs which indicate that the investment is definitely economically infeasible. The positive roots, however, represent multiple IRRs of an investment and they are actually the ones which create troubles in the DCF method. The number of positive roots can be found by *Descartes' Rule of Signs,* which can be found in any books of advanced algebra. In simple language, Descartes' Rule states that the number of positive real roots of a polynomial equation is less than or equal to the number of variations in sign of the coefficients of the equation. Therefore, a polynomial equation of i expressed in the form of:

$$k_0 i^n + k_0 i^{n-1} + \ldots + k_{n-1} i + k_n = 0 \tag{3.5}$$

where k_1, k_2, ... k_{n-1}, k_n are coefficients, can itself reveal the maximum number of positive roots without actually being solved.

If all the NCFs are known (or estimated) for an investment, equation (3.4) can be transformed algebraically into the form of equation (3.5).

Consider, for instance, the NCFs as shown in Table 3.2 by substituting the values of NCFs into equation (3.4), we obtain:

$$\frac{-10,000}{1} + \frac{4,000}{1+i} + \frac{4,500}{(1+i)^2} + \frac{5,000}{(1+i)^3} = 0 \tag{3.6}$$

Equation (3.6) can be transformed algebraically as follows:

$$-10,000(1+i)^3 + 4,000(1+i)^2 + 4,500(1+i) + 5,000 = 0$$

i.e. $-10,000 - 30,000i - 30,000i^2 - 10,000i^3 + 4,000$
$\quad + 8,000i + 4,000i^2 + 4,500 + 4,500i + 5,000 = 0$

i.e. $10,000i^3 + 26,000i^2 + 17,500i - 3,500 = 0 \tag{3.7}$

Observe that equation (3.7) is of the form represented generally by equation (3.5).

The sequence of the signs of the coefficients in equation (3.7) is:

$+ , + , + , -$

There is only one variation of sign, and hence, by Descartes' Rule, equation (3.7) has at most one positive root. Hence 16.3% (solution of Example 3.1) is the only possible IRR, and there is no multiple root problem in this case.

Fortunately, the practical situation of most project cash flows usually has the capital costs incurred at the beginning of the project and the benefits recovered gradually over its lifetime. This means that the net cash flow at the beginning, i.e. NCF_0 (or sometimes NCF_1 and NCF_2 as well if the project is big) is negative (or are negative), and thereafter, they become positive all the way down. There is a very rare chance practically that the positive and negative NCFs fluctuate vigorously over the project life (i.e. the case of Table 3.4). For this reason, the number of variations in sign of the coefficients in equation (3.5), which in fact is another form of expression of equation (3.4), would normally be one, or in some rare cases, two. Thus, the number of positive roots, i.e. IRRs, obtained would normally be one, or in some cases, two.

In view of the fact that the IRR criterion will continue to be used by many decision makers, those who use it must exercise due care with the multiple IRR problem associated with the DCF method, especially when the NCFs show frequent changes of positive and negative values.

Let us take a further look of an example with NCFs with more than one variation in sign as shown in Example 3.5.

Example 3.5

An investor invested $2,000 in year 0 and $12,000 in year 2. The incomes were $10,000 in year 1 and $4,000 in year 2. Find the rate of return of this investment.

Solution 3.5

The cash flows of the investment and the NCFs are shown in Table 3.10 below:

Table 3.10 Cash flows of the investment

End of Year	Cash out	Cash in	NCF
0	2,000		−2,000
1		10,000	+10,000
2	12,000	4,000	−8,000

There are two variations in sign and therefore it is possible that there are two IRRs.

We can find the IRRs by algebraic method:

$$\frac{NCF_0}{1}+\frac{NCF_1}{1+i}+\frac{NCF_2}{(1+i)^2}=0$$

i.e. $$-2,000+\frac{10,000}{1+i}-\frac{8,000}{(1+i)^2}=0$$

$$-2000-4,000i-2,000i^2+10,000+10,000i-8,000=0$$
$$2,000i^2-6,000=0$$

or $$i(i-3)=0$$

Therefore, $i=0$ (i.e. IRR = 0%) or $i=3$ (i.e. IRR = 300%).

The NPWs for a range of i values can be calculated using the formula:

$$NPW=-2,000+\frac{10,000}{1+i}-\frac{8,000}{(1+i)^2}$$

and the results are shown below:

i	0%	50%	100%	150%	200%	250%	300%
NPW	0	1,111	1,000	720	444	204	0

The graph of NPW versus i of this investment is shown in Fig. 3.5.

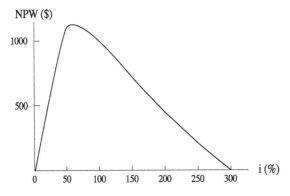

Fig. 3.5 Multiple IRRs graph (NPW vs. *i*)

Readers can observe that the shape of the graph in Fig. 3.5 is very different from that of Fig. 3.2. The latter is the shape of the graph of an investment with one IRR (or one variation in sign for the NCFs).

In Example 3.5, the IRRs are found to be 0% or 300%, and it seems that these results are meaningless. By looking at the NPW vs. *i* graph (Fig. 3.5) together with the NCFs in Table 3.10, we can guess that the rate of return of this investment should be a positive value (but it cannot be as high as 300%), since the NPWs appear to be positive at most values of *i*. Therefore, in such a case, it seems that IRR fails to give us a reasonable indication on the rate of return of the investment. In the next section, readers will be introduced to a new financial indicator, the *external rate of return* (ERR), which is used as a surrogate for the IRR.

3.6 External Rate of Return (ERR)

In the evaluation of ERR, we have to restructure the cash flows such that there is only one variation in sign. In order to do so, we have to make use of a desirable rate of return, say, 12% (the desirable rate of return is the pre-determined *i* in the examples in the other chapters). For the NCFs of Table 3.10, the income of $10,000 at the end of year 1 is assumed to be reinvested at the desirable rate of return of 12%. So, we have $11,200 at the end of year 2. The NCF at the end of year 2 now becomes $3,200 (i.e. $11,200 − $8,000). The restructured NCFs therefore are:

End of Year	NCF
0	−2,000
1	0
2	3,200

The IRR of these restructured NCFs is 26.5%, and we do not call this IRR any more but call it ERR, the external rate of return. Since this ERR is greater than 12% (the desirable rate of return), the investment is considered to be viable.

We can generalize such an approach by restructuring any cash flow patterns in such a way so that only one variation in sign appears in the restructured NCFs. Now, let us look at a further example.

Example 3.6

Find the external rate of return of the NCFs in Table 3.11 with 5 variations in sign and see if it is a viable investment given that the minimum desirable rate of return is 10%.

Table 3.11 NCFs of the investment of Example 3.6

End of Year	NCF (million $)
0	−15
1	+12
2	+13
3	−30
4	+6
5	+7
6	+8
7	−25
8	+9
9	+10
10	+11

Solution 3.6

We can see that the NCFs in this example (Table 3.11) is of a pattern like those in Table 3.4, which is undesirable for the calculation of an apparently meaningful IRR. So, we must firstly restructure the NCFs to a pattern like those in Table 3.3 in order to facilitate the calculation of a rate of return.

The restructuring can be done in three steps as follows:

Step 1 in restructuring the NCFs

We want to eliminate the negative NCF (−30) at the end of year 3 by combining the three NCFs at the end of years 1, 2 and 3. The incomes of 12 and 13 at the end of years 1 and 2 respectively are assumed to be reinvested at the desirable rate of return of of 10%.

The NCF at the end of year 3 becomes:

$$12(1 + 0.1)^2 + 13(1 + 0.1) - 30 = -1.18$$

The NCFs in Table 3.11 can be restructured as shown in Table 3.12.

Table 3.12 Restructured NCFs after Step 1

End of Year	NCF (million $)
0	-15
1	0
2	0
3	-1.18
4	+6
5	+7
6	+8
7	-25
8	+9
9	+10
10	+11

Step 2 in restructuring the NCFs

Then, the NCFs at the end of years 3, 4, 5, 6 and 7 can be restructured in a similar way by the use of the desirable rate of return of of 10% again. The NCF at the end of year 7 becomes:

$$-1.18(1 + 0.1)^4 + 6(1 + 0.1)^3 + 7(1 + 0.1)^2 + 8(1 + 0.1) - 25 = -1.47$$

The NCFs in Table 3.12 can restructured as shown in Table 3.13.

Table 3.13 Restructured NCFs after Step 2

End of Year	NCF (million $)
0	-15
1	0
2	0
3	0
4	0
5	0
6	0
7	-1.47
8	+9
9	+10
10	+11

Step 3 in structuring the NCFs

In order to eliminate the negative NCF at the end of year 7, the NCF at the end of year 8 can be, using the desirable rate of 10%, restructured as:

$-1.47(1 + 0.1) + 9 = 7.38$

The final restructured NCFs are shown in Table 3.14.

Table 3.14 Restructured NCFs after Step 3

End of Year	NCF (million $)
0	-15
1	0
2	0
3	0
4	0
5	0
6	0
7	0
8	+7.38
9	+10
10	+11

The IRR of such NCFs is calculated to be 7.3%, and therefore the ERR of this investment is 7.3%. Since the ERR is smaller than 10% (the desirable rate of return), we can conclude that the investment is not viable.

In Example 3.6, although there are five variations in sign in the NCFs, the shape of the NPW v. i graph does not have a strange shape like that in Example 3.5 (see Fig. 3.5), but have quite a "normal" shape like that of Figure 3.2. We can plot the graph by firstly finding the NPWs for a range of i values.

i	0%	2.5%	5%	7.5%	10%	15%	20%	25%	30%
NPW	6.00	2.70	0.22	−1.65	−3.08	−4.99	−6.12	−6.80	−7.23

The NPW vs. i graph is shown in Fig. 3.6. From the graph, we can see that the IRR is 5.3%. Strictly speaking, we do not need to find an ERR for this particular example of investment because, unlike Example 3.5, an IRR, which is apparently meaningful, can be obtained from the usual method of calculating the IRR. Hence, it is not always necessary to find an ERR for situations of NCFs with more than one sign variations.

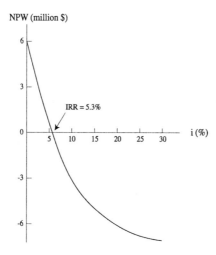

Fig. 3.6 NPW vs. *i* graph for the investment of Example 3.6

For NCFs with multiple sign changes, a graph of the behavior of NPW vs. *i* (e.g. Figs. 3.5 and 3.6) should be drawn first to see whether or not only one IRR (reasonable IRR within one's common sense) shows up on the graph, or in other words, whether or not the graph looks like Fig. 3.2. If it does, then use the "normal method" to calculate the IRR, but if this is not the situation, then the NCFs should be restructured to a form such that only one variation of sign appears, and the ERR is then calculated and used to make investment decisions.

3.7 A New Perspective on Multiple IRRs

Professor Gordon B. Hazen of Northwestern University, USA, recently published his paper "A New Perspective on Multiple Internal Rates of Return" in Vol. 48, No. 1 (2003) of *The Engineering Economist*. He discovered that when there are multiple (or even complex-valued) IRRs, each of them has a meaningful interpretation as a rate of return on its own underlying investment stream. This discovery is contradictory to the previous consensus that some multiple IRRs are meaningless (see Example 3.5). On the contrary, Professor Hazen stated that no matter which IRR is chosen under the multiple IRRs situation, the cash flow acceptance or rejection decision will be the same and consistent with NPW. We will see below in detail this great discovery of Professor Hazen.

3.7.1 Investment streams

For every cash flow (or net cash flow) situation, there are n *investment streams* (n = the number of periods considered) associated with it. Let us see Table 3.15.

Table 3.15 NCF stream and "investment stream"

End of period	Cash-out (invest)	Cash-in (receive)	NCF
0	C_0		$-C_0$
1	C_1	$(1+k)C_0$	$(1+k)C_0 - C_1$
2	C_2	$(1+k)C_1$	$(1+k)C_1 - C_2$
.	.	.	.
.	.	.	.
.	.	.	.
t	C_t	$(1+k)C_{t-1}$	$(1+k)C_{t-1} - C_t$
.	.	.	.
.	.	.	.
.	.	.	.
$n-1$	C_{n-1}	$(1+k)C_{n-2}$	$(1+k)C_{n-2} - C_{n-1}$
n	0	$(1+k)C_{n-1}$	$(1+k)C_{n-1}$

If we have a NCF stream like the one shown in Table 3.15, k is an IRR by definition, since the NCF is calculated based on a constant per period rate of return k. The cash-out stream ($C_0, C_1, C_2, \ldots, C_{n-1}, 0$) is called an *investment stream* associated with this NCF stream. Since there are n numbers of k (IRR) in theory, whether real positive, real negative or complex valued, there should be n numbers of investment streams associated with a NCF stream (with n periods). The relationship of the NCF stream and the investment stream is given by:

$$NCF_0 = -C_0$$
$$NCF_t = (1+k)C_{t-1} - C_t$$
$$NCF_n = (1+k)C_{n-1}$$

or $C_0 = -NCF_0$
$$C_t = (1+k)C_{t-1} - NCF_t$$
$$C_n = 0$$

3.7.2 "Pure investment stream" and "pure borrowing stream"

The investment stream $(C_0, C_1, C_2, \ldots, C_{n-1}, 0)$ defined in Section 3.7.1 can be classified as a *pure investment stream* or a *pure borrowing stream*. For a pure investment stream, the project is viable only if $k >$ the desirable rate of return, and vice versa. For a pure borrowing stream, the project is viable only if $k <$ the desirable rate of return, and vice versa. We will use the NCF stream in Table 3.10 to illustrate this.

Since the NCF in Table 3.10 has 2 IRRs, there are 2 investment streams associated with it as shown in Table 3.15. The desirable rate of return, as used before, is 12%.

Table 3.15 The two investment streams associated with NCFs of Table 3.10

	C_0	C_1	C_2	NPW at $i = 12\%$
Stream 1 $(k = 0)$	C_0 $= -NCF_0$ $= 2,000$	C_1 $= (1+k)(2,000)$ $- NCF_1$ $= -8,000$	C_2 $= (1+k)(-8,000)$ $- NCF_2$ $= 0$	$-4,592$
Stream 2 $(k = 300\%)$	C_0 $= -NCF_0$ $= 2,000$	C_1 $= (1+k)(2,000)$ $- NCF_1$ $= -2,000$	C_2 $= (1+k)(-2,000)$ $- NCF_2$ $= 0$	$+191$

From Table 3.15, we can see that the investment stream 1 $(k = 0)$ is a pure borrowing stream, because its NPW at $i = 12\%$ (the desirable rate of return) is negative. When $k = 0$ is compared with 12%, and because in this case $k <$ the desirable rate of return, we can conclude that the project is viable, according to the aforesaid criterion of a pure borrowing stream. The investment stream 2 $(k = 300\%)$ is a pure investment stream, because its NPW at $i = 12\%$ is positive. When $k = 300\%$ is compared with 12%, and because in this case $k >$ the desirable rate of return, we can also conclude that the project is viable, according to the aforesaid criterion of a pure investment stream. This result is consistent with the positive NPW (equal to $+551$) of the NCF stream calculated with $i = 12\%$.

Therefore, as Professor Hazen said, these multiple IRRs are meaningful, explainable and non-contradictory, and are consistent with the NPW evaluation of the NCF stream at the desirable rate of return. The problem of multiple IRRs, universally regarded as a fatal flaw for the IRR method, is not really a flaw at all, and can be dealt with conceptually and procedurally as illustrated above.

3.7.3 A further example

Page 186 (Section 7.6 of Chapter 7) of the book *Engineering Economy: Applying Theory to Practice*, written by T.G. Eschenbach (Chicago: Irwin, 1995) presents the example as shown in Table 3.16.

Table 3.16 NCF stream presented by T. G. Eschenbach

End of period	NCF ($ × 100)
0	−400
1	300
2	225
3	150
4	75
5	0
6	−75
7	−150
8	−225

There are two variations of sign for the NCF stream and hence there are two positive real IRRs, 10.43% and 26.31%, for the NCF stream of Table 3.16. If the desirable rate of return is, say, 8%. The NPW of the NCF at $i = 8\%$ is −11.5, that is, a negative value, meaning that the project is not viable. However, since the IRRs 10.43% or 26.31% are both greater than 8%, the project looks like to be a viable one. Hence, it seems that the multiple IRRs calculated are meaningless. Previously, decision makers would resort to using the ERR method as described in Section 6 of this chapter for such a situation. However, we can now view this problem with a new perspective. The two investment streams using $k = 10.43\%$ and 26.31% are shown in Table 3.17.

We can see from Table 3.17 that both investment streams are pure borrowing streams because both have negative NPWs at $i = 8\%$. For both pure borrowing streams, $k = 10.34\%$ and $k = 26.31\%$ are both greater than the desirable rate of return 8%, and therefore the project is not viable. This result is consistent with the negative NPW (equal to −11.5 as mentioned earlier) calculated with $i = 8\%$, the desirable rate of return.

3. Discount Cash Flow Method   55

Table 3.17 Investment streams associated with NCFs of Table 3.16 and NPW
calculated with the desirable rate of return = 8%

	C_0	C_1	C_2	C_3	C_4	C_5	C_6	C_7	C_8	NPW $i = 8\%$
Stream 1 $k = 10.43\%$	400	142	−69	−226	−324	−358	−320	−204	0	−510
Stream 2 $k = 26.31\%$	400	205	34	−107	−210	−265	−260	−178	0	−68

If the desirable rate of return for this problem changes from 8% to 15%, then the IRR (26.31%) exceeds the desirable rate (15%) but the other (10.43%) does not. For such a case, one stream will remain to be a pure borrowing stream, while the other one will become a pure investment stream. This is shown in Table 3.18.

Table 3.18 Investment streams associated with NCFs of Table 3.16 and NPW
calculated with the desirable rate of return = 15%

	C_0	C_1	C_2	C_3	C_4	C_5	C_6	C_7	C_8	NPW $i = 15\%$
Stream 1 $k = 10.43\%$	400	142	−69	−226	−324	−358	−320	−204	0	−256
Stream 2 $k = 26.31\%$	400	205	34	−107	−210	−265	−260	−178	0	+102

From stream 1, we can see that it is a pure borrowing stream. Since $k = 10.43\% < 15\%$, the desirable rate of return, the project is viable. From stream 2, we can see that it is a pure investment stream. Since $k = 26.31\% > 15\%$, the project is viable. There is never a contradiction. Also, the result is consistent with the positive NPW (equal to +10.1) for the NCF stream obtained when the calculation is based on i = 15%.

3.8 Problems

1. How does the discount cash flow (DCF) method of calculation auto-matically allow for depreciation?

2. By the DCF method, find the IRR of each of the following 3 alternatives and hence determine which one is the best to adopt.

End of year	Alternative A NCF	Alternative B NCF	Alternative C NCF
0	-$30,000	-$30,000	-$30,000
1	4,000	9,000	10,000
2	5,000	9,000	8,000
3	6,000	9,000	7,000
4	7,000	9,000	7,000
5	8,000		6,000
6	9,000		

(*Note*: In this exercise, the alternative with the highest IRR is the best to adopt, and there is no need to compare the alternatives based on the same time horizon as illustrated in Examples 2.3 and 2.4 in Chapter 2. The reason for this has been slightly discussed in this chapter and will be further discussed in Chapter 5.)

3. (a) Why can there be multiple IRRs for a single pattern of cash flows?
   (b) Under what cash flows situation can a single IRR be obtained? Why?

4. Use the ERR (external rate of return) method to find whether the NCF stream of Table 3.16 is viable when the desirable rate of return is (a) 8% and (b) 15%.

4. INFLATION

4.1 Effect of Inflation in Equivalence Calculation

In the previous three chapters, project appraisals were performed in an assumed inflation-free world. The currency was assumed to be stable and the purchasing power of money would not decline but remain unchanged over time.

In an inflation-free world, the NPW is usually represented mathematically by:

$$\text{NPW} = \frac{\text{NCF}_0}{1} + \frac{\text{NCF}_1}{1+i} + \frac{\text{NCF}_2}{(1+i)^2} + \cdots + \frac{\text{NCF}_n}{(1+i)^n} \tag{4.1}$$

(The above equation is in fact equation (3.3) or equation (3.3a) of Chapter 3).

But if we come back to the real world, which is not inflation-free, adjustment to the above equation (4.1) is necessary.

Now, let $\quad f_1$ = inflation expressed as a percentage in year 1
$\qquad f_2$ = inflation expressed as a percentage in year 2

.

.

.

$\qquad f_n$ = inflation expressed as a percentage in year n

then, $\quad$ NPW (in real term)

$$= \frac{\text{NCF}_0}{1} + \frac{\text{NCF}_1}{(1+i)(1+f_1)} + \frac{\text{NCF}_2}{(1+i)^2(1+f_1)(1+f_2)} + \cdots$$

$$+ \frac{\text{NCF}_n}{(1+i)^n(1+f_1)+(1+f_2)+\cdots+(1+f_n)} \tag{4.2}$$

The effect of i (the time value of money) is to devalue the future cash flows. The effect of f (inflation), similar to i, also devalues the future cash flows. $(1 + i)$ and $(1 + f)$, therefore, are put together as factors in the denominator in equation (4.2).

If inflation is expected to be the same in every year within the life of the project, then:

$$f_1 = f_2 = \ldots = f_n = f$$

and equation (4.2) will become

$$\text{NPW (real)} = \frac{NCF_0}{1} + \frac{NCF_1}{(1+i)(1+f)} + \frac{NCF_2}{(1+i)^2(1+f)^2} + \cdots + \frac{NCF_n}{(1+i)^n(1+f)^n} \quad (4.3)$$

Example 4.1

Table 4.1 Actual NCFs from 1991 to 1996 with known inflation in respective years

End of year	NCF	Inflation
1991	−90,000	
1992	28,000	10%
1993	32,000	12%
1994	37,000	11%
1995	45,000	13%
1996	50,000	9%

Table 4.1 shows the *actual* net cash flows from 1991 to 1996. The figures were actually obtained from the accounting records of the past five years. Inflation rates published by the government were 10%, 12%, 11 %, 13%, 9% each year from 1992 to 1996 respectively. Find the NPW in real term if i (the real discount rate) is taken as 14%.

Solution 4.1

$$
\begin{aligned}
\text{NPW (real)} &= \frac{-90,000}{1} + \frac{28,000}{(1+14\%)(1+10\%)} + \frac{32,000}{(1+14\%)^2(1+10\%)(1+12\%)} \\
&\quad + \frac{37,000}{(1+14\%)^3(1+10\%)(1+12\%)(1+11\%)} \\
&\quad + \frac{45,000}{(1+14\%)^4(1+10\%)(1+12\%)(1+11\%)(1+13\%)} \\
&\quad + \frac{50,000}{(1+14\%)^5(1+10\%)(1+12\%)(1+11\%)(1+13\%)(1+9\%)} \\
&= -90,000 + 22,329 + 19,986 + 18,262 + 17,242 + 15,417 \\
&= \$3,236
\end{aligned}
$$

4.2 Apparent Rate of Return (i')

In Section 2 of Chapter 1, the concepts of *real rate* and *apparent rate* were introduced to the reader. If i' is taken as the apparent rate, it can be easily understood that the cash flows should be discounted by i' and that the real NPW should be calculated in the following manner:

$$\text{NPW (real)} = \frac{\text{NCF}_0}{1} + \frac{\text{NCF}_1}{1+i'} + \frac{\text{NCF}_2}{(1+i')^2} + \cdots + \frac{\text{NCF}_n}{(1+i')^n} \qquad (4.4)$$

By comparing equations (4.3) and (4.4), it is easily observed that:

$$(1 + i') = (1 + i)(1 + f) \qquad (4.5)$$

or $i' = (1 + i)(1 + f) - 1$ $\qquad (4.5a)$

The readers should note that equation (4.5a) has been quoted in Section 2 of Chapter 1 as equation (1.1).

Example 4.2

An item of equipment was purchased four years ago at $50,000 and it had a life of 4 years. This investment gave rise to *actual* annual cash receipts of $15,000; $20,500; $25,500 and $29,000 respectively in the past 4 years. The average rate of inflation over these years was 11 % per annum. Find the real IRR.

Solution 4.2

Let i = real IRR and i' = apparent IRR.
There are two methods in evaluating the real IRR.

Method 1: Find the real IRR directly.

End of year	(1) NCF	(2) $(pwf)^{11\%}$	(3) $(pwf)^{5\%}$	(4) $(DCF)^{5\%}$ (1) ×(2) × (3)	(5) $(pwf)10\%$	(6) $(DCF)^{10\%}$ (1) ×(2) × (5)
0	−50,000	1.00000	1.00000	−50,000	1.00000	−50,000
1	15,000	0.90090	0.95238	12,870	0.90909	12,285
2	20,500	0.81162	0.90702	15,091	0.82644	13,750
3	25,500	07.3119	0.86383	16,106	0.75131	14,008
4	29,000	0.65873	0.82270	15,716	0.68301	13,048
				9,783		3,091

$$i = 10\% + \left(\frac{3,091}{9,783-3,091}\right)(10-5)\% = 12\% \text{ (i.e. real IRR)}$$

Method 2: Find i' first and then calculate the real IRR by formula.

End of Year	(1) NCF	(2) $(pwf)^{12\%}$	(3) $(DCF)^{12\%}$ (1) × (2)	(4) $(pwf)^{20\%}$	(5) $(DCF)^{20\%}$ (1) × (4)
0	−50,000	1.00000	−50,000	1.00000	−50,000
1	15,000	0.89285	13,393	0.83333	12,500
2	20,500	0.79719	16,342	0.69444	14,236
3	25,500	0.71178	18,150	0.57870	14,757
4	29,000	0.63551	18,430	0.48225	13,985
			16,315		5,478

$$i' = 20\% + \left(\frac{5,478}{16,315-5,478}\right)(20-12)\% = 24\% \text{ (i.e. apparent IRR)}.$$

Use equation (4.5a),

$$i' = (1+i)(1+f) - 1$$

or $0.24 = (1+i)(1+0.11) - 1$

Solve for i gives $i = 12\%$ (real IRR)
Therefore, the same answer is obtained.

4.3 When to Incorporate Inflation Adjustment?

Consider a 10-years-life project having the net cash flows as shown in Table 4.2.

Table 4.2 NCFs of constant base year prices

End of year	Net cash flow
0	NCF_0
1	NCF_1
2	NCF_2
.	.
.	.
.	.
10	NCF_{10}

The NPW of the project can be calculated using equations (3.3), (3.3a) or (4.1) as follows:

$$\text{NPW} = \frac{\text{NCF}_0}{1} + \frac{\text{NCF}_1}{1+i} + \frac{\text{NCF}_2}{(1+i)^2} + \cdots + \frac{\text{NCF}_{10}}{(1+i)^{10}} \tag{4.6}$$

The NPW calculated in this manner is not apparent but real. No inflation adjustment is necessary simply because all the NCFs are based on the value of money at the time of performing the appraisal, say, 2002. This can be explained further as follows:

Table 4.3 NCFs of values at constant base year 2002

End of year	Net cash flow
0	NCF_0 (based on 2002 money)
1	NCF_1 (based on 2002 money)
2	NCF_2 (based on 2002 money)
.	.
.	.
.	.
10	NCF_{10} (based on 2002 money)

If the NCFs in Table 4.3 are used to calculate the NPW by equation (4-6), the NPW calculated is real.

If inflation were assumed to be of an average rate of $f\%$ p.a. over these 10 years, then the NCFs could be estimated (as shown in Table 4.4) as *actual* transactions in these years.

Table 4.4 NCFs of actual transactions in respective years

End of year	NCF (Actual transactions)
0	NCF_0 (based on 2002 money)
1	$\text{NCF}_1 \times (1+f)$ (based on 2003 money)
2	$\text{NCF}_2 \times (1+f)^2$ (based on 2004 money)
.	.
.	.
.	.
10	$\text{NCF}_{10} \times (1+f)^{10}$ (based on 2012 money)

In such a case, the NPW in real term should be calculated by equation (4.4) with the use of i', the apparent discount rate, as follows:

$$\frac{NPW}{(real)} = \frac{NCF_0}{1} + \frac{NCF_1 \times (1+f)}{1+i'} + \frac{NCF_2 \times (1+f)^2}{(1+i')^2} + \cdots + \frac{NCF_{10} \times (1+f)^{10}}{(1+i')^{10}}$$

(4.7)

Substituting equation (4.5) into equation (4.7), we obtain:

$$\frac{NPW}{(real)} = \frac{NCF_0}{1} + \frac{NCF_1 \times (1+f)}{(1+i')(1+f)} + \frac{NCF_2 \times (1+f)^2}{(1+i')^2(1+f)^2} + \cdots + \frac{NCF_{10} \times (1+f)^{10}}{(1+i')^{10}(1+f)^{10}}$$

$$= \frac{NCF_0}{1} + \frac{NCF_1}{(1+i')} + \frac{NCF_2}{(1+i')^2} + \cdots + \frac{NCF_{10}}{(1+i')^{10}}$$

which is identical to equation (4.6).

Therefore, it can be concluded that the evaluation of real NPW, using NCFs of *constant base year prices,* has no need to consider at all the effects of inflation. This conclusion leads to another extremely important point, which is that all the methods of project appraisal described in Chapters 1, 2 and 3 are *valid even in a world with inflation,* that is, even if the inflation-free assumption were not made. That such an assumption was made in the beginning is merely for the sake of easy explanation.

In Section 5 of Chapter 1, bank loan repayment methods were discussed. The present worths calculated as shown on page 13 were real. Although the loan repayments were actual transactions (not constant base year prices), yet the bank interest rate used to calculate the present worth was apparent (in Section 2 of Chapter 1 we have discussed that bank interest rates are apparent rates). Therefore, we were in fact using equation 4.4 to calculate the present worth on page 13, and hence the results were real. Moreover, readers should note that the result of Example 3.4 is an apparent rate, or more exactly, the bank interest rate (or the nominal rate).

Most of the project appraisals are performed with their cash flows estimated at constant base year prices, like the NCFs shown in Table 4.3, and so their results are real. For financial or economic feasibility studies of projects at the planning stage, one simply cannot have cash flow figures like those in Examples 4.1 and 4.2. One can only estimate future cash flows based on constant year prices, like those shown in Table 4.3. Let us look at a further example.

Example 4.3

It is proposed to construct a self-financing road tunnel. The criterion is that the toll paid by the vehicles over the life of the project must be sufficient to recover both the initial capital and the other costs which will be incurred over the project's life. Determine a suitable charge on each vehicle passing through the tunnel using the following estimated figures based on 2002 prices.

1. Capital cost:
   (a) Construction cost
   (b) Land cost $100,000,000
   (c) Professional fees

2. Annual OMR cost $2,500,000

3. Annual administration cost $ 5,000,000

4. Replacement cost of autopay ticket machine $ 1,000,000
                                                           every 5 years

5. Estimated annual traffic flow   10,000 vehicles per
                                                           day in the first 5
                                                           years, the growth
                                                           rate of traffic flow is
                                                           30% every 5 years.

6. Life of project   20 years

7. Required rate of return (real)   12%

8. Estimated inflation rate in the next 20 years   10% p.a. (average)

Solution 4.3

By looking at the data given, one can easily see that the money values are of constant base year prices, otherwise how can the annual OMR cost be $2,500,000 over 20 years remaining unchanged. Now let us do the calculations.

1. Initial costs $100,000,000

2. PW of annual OMR costs
   $= 2,500,000 \times (uspwf)^{n=20, i=12\%} =$ $18,673,500

3. PW of annual administration costs
   $= 5,000,000 \times (uspwf)^{n=20, i=12\%} =$ $37,347,000

4. PW of replacement costs for ticket machine
   $= 1,000,000 \times (pwf)^{n=5, i=12\%}$
   $+ 1,000,000 \times (pwf)^{n=10, i=12\%}$
   $+ 1,000,000 \times (pwf)^{n=15, i=12\%} =$ $\underline{\$1,072,080}$

Present worth of total costs = $\underline{\$157,092,580}$

Number of vehicles passing the tunnel each year in the 1st five years (i.e. year 1 to year 5)	= 10,000 × 365 = 3,650,000
Number of vehicles passing the tunnel each year in the 2nd five years (i.e. year 6 to year 10)	= (10,000 × 1.3) × 365 = 13,000 × 365 = 4,745,000
Number of vehicles passing the tunnel each year in the 3rd five years (i.e. year 11 to year 15)	= (13,000 × 1.3) × 365 = 16,900 × 365 = 6,168,500
Number of vehicles passing the tunnel each year in the 4th five years (i.e. year 16 to year 20)	= (16,900 × 1.3) × 365 = 21,970 × 365 = 8,019,050

If y = toll paid by each vehicle,
then,   PW of income in the 1st five years

$$= 3,650,000y \times (\text{uspwf})^{n=5, i=12\%} = \qquad \$13,157,155y$$

PW of income in the 2nd five years

$$= 4,745,000y \times (\text{uspwf})^{n=5, i=12\%} \times (\text{pwf})^{n=5, i=12\%} = \qquad \$9,705,323y$$

PW of income in the 3rd five years

$$= 6,168,500y \times (\text{uspwf})^{n=5, i=12\%} \times (\text{pwf})^{n=10, i=12\%} = \qquad \$7,159,194y$$

PW of income in the 4th five years

$$= 8,019,050y \times (\text{uspwf})^{n=5, i=12\%} \times (\text{pwf})^{n=15, i=12\%} = \qquad \underline{\$5,280,886y}$$

$$\text{Total} \qquad \underline{\$35,302,558y}$$

At break-even point, $157,092,580 = 35,302,558y$

$$\therefore \qquad y = \frac{157,092,580}{35,302,558} = \$4.45$$

The minimum toll paid by each vehicle initially is $4.45 in order not to lose money. A toll of, say, $5 is reasonable if one wishes to make some profit.

Note: The effect of inflation (10% p.a. on average) has not been taken account of in the above calculation. It is in fact not necessary to do so because constant base year prices are used. Inflation indeed may influence both revenues and costs to differing degrees, but such impacts are only of short duration. Usually, its effect on both revenues and costs will cancel out each other in the long run to regain a balance.

Therefore, if f = 10% p.a., simply increase the toll also 10% p.a. on average in principle (with skillful price-increase technique of course) to adjust the effect of inflation.

Mathematically:

Toll after n years $= \$4.45 \times (1 + 10\%)^n$
or $\qquad\qquad\quad = \$5.00 \times (1 + 10\%)^n$ if profit is desired
where $n = 1, 2, \ldots 20$.

Example 4.4

A promoter has received two tenders for the construction of a new apartment house. The details of the tenders are:

Tender A: Contract sum $30,000,000; contract period 15 months; payment made at the end of every quarter, i.e. a total of 5 uniform payments with each payment equal to 20% of the contract sum.

Tender B: Contract sum $32,000,000; contract period 12 months; payment made at the end of every quarter, i.e. a total of 4 uniform payments with each payment equal to 25% of the contract sum.

(a) Assuming that the potential rental value of the new house is $1,000,000 per month, receivable at the end of each month immediately after completion, explain by calculation why tender B should be selected by the promoter.

(b) If contract B completed the contract on schedule in the first three quarters but one month late in the last quarter (so that the payments at the end of the 4th quarter was 15% of the contract sum and that at the end of the 13th month was 10% of the same), determine the amount that should be deducted from the final payment in order to ensure adequate compensation for the promoter.

(Use the bank interest rate 12% p.a. to calculate the compensation and also use it in determining the present worth of the two tenders.)

Solution 4.4

The interim (quarterly) payments are actual transactions and so they are *not* values at constant base year. However, since the bank interest rate (i') is used to calculate the present worth, the results obtained are real according to equation (4.4).

(a) The present worths of the two tenders are:

$$PW_A = \frac{6,000,000}{(1+0.01)^3} + \frac{6,000,000}{(1+0.01)^6} + \frac{6,000,000}{(1+0.01)^9} + \frac{6,000,000}{(1+0.01)^{12}} + \frac{6,000,000}{(1+0.01)^{15}}$$

$= 5,823,600 + 5,652,000 + 5,485,800 + 5,324,400 + 5,167,800$

$= 27,453,600$

$$PW_B = \frac{8,000,000}{(1+0.01)^3} + \frac{8,000,000}{(1+0.01)^6} + \frac{8,000,000}{(1+0.01)^9} + \frac{8,000,000}{(1+0.01)^{12}} - \frac{1,000,000}{(1+0.01)^{13}}$$

$$- \frac{1,000,000}{(1+0.01)^{14}} - \frac{1,000,000}{(1+0.01)^{15}}$$

$$= 7,764,800 + 7,536,000 + 7,314,400 + 7,099,200 - 878,700$$

$$- 870,000 - 861,300$$

$$= 27,104,400$$

Since $PW_B < PW_A$, the promoter should accept tender B.

(b) Present worth of tender B for the delayed case:

$$PW_B = \frac{8,000,000}{(1+0.01)^3} + \frac{8,000,000}{(1+0.01)^6} + \frac{8,000,000}{(1+0.01)^9} + \frac{4,800,000}{(1+0.01)^{12}} + \frac{3,200,000}{(1+0.01)^{13}}$$

$$- \frac{1,000,000}{(1+0.01)^{14}} - \frac{1,000,000}{(1+0.01)^{15}}$$

$$= 7,764,800 + 7,536,000 + 7,314,400 + 4,259,520 + 2,811,840$$

$$- 870,000 - 861,300$$

$$= 27,955,260$$

The amount that should be deducted from the final payment in order to ensure adequate compensation for the promoter

$$= (27,955,260 - 27,104,400) \times (1 + 0.01)^{13} = 850,860 \times 1.1381$$

$$= \$968,364$$

4.4 Problems

1. Under what cash flow situations should inflation adjustment be necessary and unnecessary? Give examples.

2. The following cash flows are the *actual transactions* in the respective years as indicated. The average inflation rate for those years is 8% p.a. Find the real IRR.

End of year	Cash out	Cash in
1991	$102,482	$28,863
1992		$30,972
1993		$30,972
1994		$34,586
1995		$38,461
1996		$43,313

5. Comparison of Multiple Alternatives

5.1 Comparison of Mutually Exclusive Projects

In previous chapters, the comparison of alternatives has been illustrated in Examples 2-3, 2-4, 2-8 and 3-2. It must be noted that in all these examples, either the initial costs of the alternatives are equal (as in Example 3-2 and Problem 2 of Chapter 3) or the benefits of the alternatives are deemed to be the same (as in Examples 2-3, 2-4 and 2-8). In such cases, the comparison of alternatives is relatively easy, as *the highest net annual benefit* (or *minimum annual cost*) criterion, *the highest net present worth* (or *minimum present worth of costs*) criterion, *the highest benefit-cost ratio* criterion and *the highest IRR* criterion would all yield the same conclusion. Consistent answers could be obtained whichever criteria were used.

However, for multiple alternatives (also known as mutually exclusive alternatives), i.e. those with different initial costs and different benefits as well, the conclusions drawn may not necessarily be consistent by the use of the said criteria. Let us see the following example.

Example 5.1

A flood storage reservoir is to be built for a flood control scheme. Several reservoir capacities are being considered and their benefit/cost data are shown below:

	Reservoir capacity (m^3)	Initial capital $\$ \times 10^6$	Annual OMR cost $\$ \times 10^6$	Annual benefit $\$ \times 10^6$
Alternative 1	50×10^6	50	0.4	5.6
Alternative 2	100×10^6	70	1.0	8.0
Alternative 3	150×10^6	110	1.5	10.5
Alternative 4	200×10^6	140	1.7	15.2
Alternative 5	250×10^6	180	2.0	19.0

Assuming that the project life is 30 years and that the discount rate is 6%, determine:
(a) the alternative with the highest net annual benefit,
(b) the alternative with the highest net present worth,
(c) the alternative with the highest B/C ratio, and
(d) the alternative with the highest IRR.

Solution 5.1

(a)   The net annual benefit of each alternative is calculated and shown in Table 5.1.1.

Table 5.1.1 Ranking multiple alternatives (highest net annual benefit criterion)

Alt.	Equivalent annual cost of initial capital	(1) Annual OMR cost	(2) Total annual cost (1) + (2)	(3) Annual benefit	(4) Net annual benefit (4) – (3)	(5) Rank-ing
1	$50 \times (uscrf)^{n=30, i=6\%} = 3.63$	0.4	4.03	5.6	+1.57	4
2	$70 \times (uscrf)^{n=30, i=6\%} = 5.09$	1.0	6.09	8.0	+1.91	3
3	$110 \times (uscrf)^{n=30, i=6\%} = 7.99$	1.5	9.49	10.5	+1.01	5
4	$140 \times (uscrf)^{n=30, i=6\%} = 10.17$	1.7	11.87	15.2	+3.33	2
5	$180 \times (uscrf)^{n=30, i=6\%} = 13.08$	20	15.08	19.0	**+3.92**	1

Alternative 5 has the highest net annual benefit.

(b)   The net present worth of each alternative is calculated and shown in Table 5.1.2.

Alternative 5 has the highest net present worth.

(c)   The B/C ratio of each alternative can be calculated

either by $\dfrac{\text{annual benefit}}{\text{annual cost}}$ or $\dfrac{\text{P.W. of benefits}}{\text{P.W. of costs}}$

The results are shown in Table 5.1.3.

Table 5.1.2 Ranking multiple alternatives (highest net present worth criterion)

Alt.	(1) Initial capital	(2) Present worth of OMR costs	(3) Present worth of total costs (1) + (2)	(4) Present worth of benefits	(5) Net present worth (4) − (3)	Rank-ing
1	50	$0.4 \times (uspwf)^{n=30,i=6\%}$ = 5.51	55.51	$5.6 \times (uspwf)^{n=30,i=6\%}$ = 77.08	+21.57	4
2	70	$1.0 \times (uspwf)^{n=30,i=6\%}$ = 13.77	83.77	$8.0 \times (uspwf)^{n=30,i=6\%}$ = 110.12	+26.35	3
3	110	$1.5 \times (uspwf)^{n=30,i=6\%}$ = 20.65	130.65	$10.5 \times (uspwf)^{n=30,i=6\%}$ = 144.53	+13.88	5
4	140	$1.7 \times (uspwf)^{n=30,i=6\%}$ = 23.40	163.40	$15.2 \times (uspwf)^{n=30,i=6\%}$ = 209.23	+45.83	2
5	180	$2.0 \times (uspwf)^{n=30,i=6\%}$ = 27.53	207.53	$19.0 \times (uspwf)^{n=30,i=6\%}$ = 261.53	**+54.00**	1

Table 5.1.3 Ranking multiple alternatives (highest B/C ratio criterion)

Alternatve	B/C		Ranking
1	$\dfrac{5.6}{4.03}$	or $\dfrac{77.08}{55.51}$ = **1.39**	1
2	$\dfrac{8.0}{6.09}$	or $\dfrac{110.12}{83.77}$ = 1.31	2
3	$\dfrac{10.5}{9.49}$	or $\dfrac{144.53}{130.65}$ = 1.11	5
4	$\dfrac{15.2}{11.87}$	or $\dfrac{209.23}{163.4}$ = 1.28	3
5	$\dfrac{19.0}{15.08}$	or $\dfrac{261.53}{207.53}$ = 1.26	4

Alternative 1 has the highest B/C ratio.

(d) The IRR of each alternative is shown in Table 5.1.4, the detailed calculation of which is left to the readers.

Table 5.1.4 Ranking multiple alternatives (highest IRR criterion)

Alternative	IRR	Ranking
1	**9.8%**	1
2	9.3%	2
3	7.2%	5
4	8.9%	3
5	8.7%	4

Alternative 1 has the highest IRR.

It can be observed that criteria (a) and (b) are consistent with each other and so are criteria (c) and (d). The first two criteria, however, are not consistent with the last two.

Readers should note that the net annual benefit and the net present worth criteria are *always* consistent with each other, and so are the B/C ratio and the IRR criteria, in comparing whatever alternatives.

5.2 Net Present Worth versus IRR

In the previous section, we have seen an example of the comparison of multiple alternatives in which conclusions from net present worth criterion and IRR criterion are inconsistent. This is, however, not necessarily always true. The results from these two criteria can sometimes be consistent. Let us now see another example.

Example 5.2

Repeat doing Example 5.1 if i is changed from 6% p.a. to 9% p.a.

Solution 5.2

(a) The net annual benefit of each alternative is calculated and shown in Table 5.2.1.

Alternative 1 has the highest net annual benefit.

(b) The net present worth of each alternative is calculated and shown in Table 5.2.2.

Alternative 1 has the highest net present worth.

Table 5.2.1 Ranking multiple alternatives (highest net annual benefit criterion)

Alt	Equivalent annual cost of initial capital	Annual OMR cost	Total annual cost	Annual benefit	Net annual benefit	Ranking
1	4.87	0.4	5.27	5.6	**+0.33**	1
2	6.81	1.0	7.81	8.0	+0.19	2
3	10.71	1.5	12.21	10.5	−1.71	5
4	13.62	1.7	15.32	15.2	−0.12	3
5	17.52	2.0	19.52	19.0	−0.52	4

Table 5.2.2 Ranking multiple alternatives (highest net present worth criterion)

Alt	Initial capital	Present worth of OMR costs	Present worth of total costs	Present worth of benefits	Net present worth	Ranking
1	50	4.11	54.11	57.53	**+3.42**	1
2	70	10.27	80.27	82.19	+1.92	2
3	110	15.41	125.41	107.87	−17.54	5
4	140	17.47	157.47	156.16	−1.31	3
5	180	20.55	200.55	195.20	−5.35	4

(c)   The B/C ratio of each alternative is calculated and shown in Table 5.2.3.

Alternative 1 has the highest B/C ratio.

(d)   The IRR of each alternative is shown in Table 5.2.4, which is similar to Table 5.1.4.

Alternative 1 has the highest IRR.

Therefore, we can see that the ranking of the first two criteria are consistent with the last two if a discount rate of 9% p.a. is used instead of 6% p.a. This phenomenon can be explained by Fig. 5.1. In Section 3 of Chapter 3, the typical shape of a NPW-i curve was discussed. The NPW-i curves of Alternatives A and B are plotted in Fig. 5.1.

Table 5.2.3 Ranking multiple alternatives (highest B/C ratio criterion)

Alt	B/C		Ranking
1	$\dfrac{5.6}{5.27}$ or $\dfrac{57.53}{54.11}$	= **1.06**	1
2	$\dfrac{8.0}{7.81}$ or $\dfrac{82.19}{80.27}$	= 1.02	2
3	$\dfrac{10.5}{12.21}$ or $\dfrac{107.87}{125.41}$	= 0.86	5
4	$\dfrac{15.2}{15.32}$ or $\dfrac{156.16}{157.47}$	= 0.99	3
5	$\dfrac{19.0}{19.52}$ or $\dfrac{195.20}{200.55}$	= 0.97	4

Table 5.24 Ranking multiple alternatives (highest IRR criterion)

All	IRR	Ranking
1	**9.8%**	1
2	9.3%	2
3	7.2%	5
4	8.9%	3
5	8.7%	4

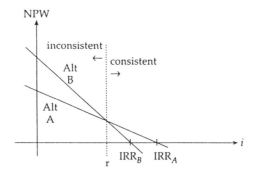

Fig. 5.1 NPW vs. i curves for multiple alternatives.

Alternative A is better than Alternative B if IRR criterion in used since IRR_A is greater than IRR_B. The B/C ratio calculated using any value of i would also give the same ranking as both IRR and B/C ratio express the rate of return of the alternatives. For $i > r$ (see Fig. 5.1), the NPW criterion is consistent with the IRR (or B/C) criterion as NPW_A is greater than NPW_B. For $i < r$, however, NPW_A is less than NPW_B and hence the NPW criterion would be inconsistent with the IRR (or B/C) criterion. Obviously, in our example, 6% is less than r and 9% is greater than r. The value of r can be evaluated and the calculation is left to the readers.

5.3 The Incremental Analysis

Neither the highest direct B/C ratio nor direct IRR always corresponds to the highest NPW of multiple alternatives. The incremental benefit-cost ratio ($\Delta B/\Delta C$) analysis and the incremental internal rate of return (ΔIRR) analysis, which are to be thoroughly discussed below, however, will be consistent with the highest NPW criterion.

5.3.1 The incremental B/C analysis

The incremental B/C ratio (i.e. $\Delta B/\Delta C$) is defined as:

$$\frac{\text{benefit of Alt } k - \text{benefit of Alt } (k-1)}{\text{cost of Alt } k - \text{cost of Alt } (k-1)}$$

if there are N multiple alternatives for $2 \leqq k \leqq N$.

In the incremental B/C analysis, the alternatives are so arranged that their annual costs (or present worth of cost) are in increasing order, that is, alternative 1 has the lowest annual cost (or the lowest present worth of cost) and alternative N the highest. The best alternative is determined using the criterion that no increase in cost is justifiable unless there is at least an equal increase in benefit. It means that:

if $\Delta B/\Delta C > 1 \Rightarrow$ Alt k is better than Alt $(k-1)$,

or   if $\Delta B/\Delta C < 1 \Rightarrow$ Alt $(k-1)$ is better than Alt k.

Example 5.3

Use incremental B/C analysis to select the best alternatives out of the five as given in Example 5.1.

Solution 5.3

Alternatives 1 to 5 have already been arranged in an increasing order of annual costs. Therefore, we firstly compare alternatives 1 and 2.

$$\left(\frac{\Delta B}{\Delta C}\right)_{2-1} = \frac{\text{Annual benefit of Alt 2} - \text{Annual benefit of Alt 1}}{\text{Annual cost of Alt 2} - \text{Annual cost of Alt 1}}$$

$$= \frac{8.0 - 5.6}{6.09 - 4.03} = \frac{2.4}{2.06}$$

$$= 1.17 > 1 \Rightarrow \text{Alternative 2 is better than alternative 1.}$$

Therefore, Alternative 1 is out. Next, we compare Alternatives 2 and 3.

$$\left(\frac{\Delta B}{\Delta C}\right)_{3-2} = \frac{10.5 - 8.0}{9.49 - 6.09} = \frac{2.5}{3.4} = 0.74 < 1$$

Thus Alternative 2 is better than Alternative 3 and Alternative 3 is out. Next, we compare Alternatives 2 and 4.

$$\left(\frac{\Delta B}{\Delta C}\right)_{4-2} = \frac{15.2 - 8.0}{11.87 - 6.09} = 1.25 > 1$$

Thus Alternative 4 is better than Alternative 2 and Alternative 2 is out. Then, the last step is to compare Alternatives 4 and 5.

$$\left(\frac{\Delta B}{\Delta C}\right)_{5-4} = \frac{19.0 - 15.2}{15.08 - 11.87} = 1.18 > 1$$

Thus Alternative 5 is better than Alternative 4. Hence, we can conclude that Alternative 5 is the best. This is consistent with the highest net annual benefit criterion and the highest net present worth criterion.

5.3.2   The incremental IRR analysis

The ΔIRR is the IRR calculated from ΔNCF where ΔNCF = (NCF of Alt k) – (NCF of Alt $k - 1$).

Similar to the $\Delta B/\Delta C$ analysis, the alternative with the lowest initial capital cost is arranged as the first alternative and the one with the highest initial capital cost as the last. The best alternative is determined by comparing each ΔIRR with a predetermined discount rate i (or a desirable rate of return) such that:

if ΔIRR $> i \Rightarrow$ Alt k is better than Alt $(k - 1)$,

or   if ΔIRR $< i \Rightarrow$ Alt $(k - 1)$ is better than Alt k.

Example 5.4

Use incremental IRR analysis to select the best alternative out of the five as given in Example 5.1.

Solution 5.4

In this example, the predetermined i is 6% p.a.

Firstly, compare Alternatives 1 and 2.

End of year	NCF$_1$		End of year	NCF$_2$		End of year	(ΔNCF)$_{2-1}$
0	−50		0	−70		0	−20
1	+5.2		1	+7.0		1	+1.8
2	+5.2	and	2	+7.0	$\Rightarrow$	2	+1.8
.			.			.	
.			.			.	
.			.			.	
30	+5.2		30	+7.0		30	+1.8

ΔIRR is calculated to be 8.1 %, which is greater than 6%. Thus Alternative 2 is better than Alternative 1 and Alternative 1 is out.

Next, compare Alternatives 2 and 3.

End of year	NCF$_2$		End of year	NCF$_3$		End of year	(ΔNCF)$_{3-2}$
0	−70		0	−110		0	−40
1	+7.0		1	+9.0		1	+2.0
2	+7.0	and	2	+9.0	$\Rightarrow$	2	+2.0
.			.			.	
.			.			.	
.			.			.	
30	+7.0		30	+9.0		30	+2.0

ΔIRR is calculated to be 2.8%, which is smaller than 6%. Thus Alternative 2 is better than alternative 3 and Alternative 3 is out.

Next, compare Alternatives 2 and 4.

End of year	NCF$_2$		End of year	NCF$_4$		End of year	(ΔNCF)$_{4-2}$
0	−70		0	−140		0	−70
1	+7.0		1	+13.5		1	+6.5
2	+7.0	and	2	+13.5	$\Rightarrow$	2	+6.5
.			.			.	
.			.			.	
.			.			.	
30	+7.0		30	+13.5		30	+6.5

ΔIRR is calculated to be 8.5%, which is greater than 6%. Thus Alternative 4 is better than Alternative 2 and Alternative 2 is out.

Lastly, compare Alternatives 4 and 5.

End of year	NCF_4		End of year	NCF_5		End of year	$(\Delta NCF)_{5-4}$
0	−140		0	−180		0	−40
1	+13.5		1	+17.0		1	+3.5
2	+13.5	and	2	+17.0	$\Rightarrow$	2	+3.5
.			.			.	
.			.			.	
.			.			.	
30	+13.5		30	+17.0		30	+3.5

ΔIRR is calculated to be 7.8% , which is greater than 6%. Thus Alternative 5 is better than alternative 4.

Hence, we can conclude that alternative 5 is the best. This is also consistent with the highest net present worth criterion, but is inconsistent with the direct IRR criterion.

Observe that if the predetermined i were taken as 9% instead of 6% (Example 5.2), then the result of the ΔIRR analysis will be consistent with the results obtained by all the other criteria. The readers can verify this point by themselves.

The two incremental analysis can be summarized in Table 5.3.

Table 5.3 Comparing ΔB/ΔC and ΔIRR analysis

	ΔB/ΔC analysis	ΔIRR analysis
1	Start with the project with lowest cost and proceed in an increasing order of project cost.	Start, with the project with lowest initial capital outlay and proceed in an increasing order of initial cash-out.
2	Y is better than X if: $$\frac{\text{Benefit of Y} - \text{Benefit of Y}}{\text{Cost of Y} - \text{Cost of Y}} > 1,$$ and vice-versa.	Y is better than X if: $\Delta IRR_{Y-X} >$ the desirable rate of return, and vice-versa.
3	Repeat step 2 until all alternatives have been compared.	Repeat step 2 until all alternatives have been compared.

5.4 Criteria for Comparison of Multiple Alternatives

Before going further, let us summarize the foregoing discussion:

Summary

	Methods of 1st set	Methods of 2nd set
1	Criteria: (1) Highest net annual benefit (2) Highest net present worth (3) ΔB/ΔC analysis (4) ΔIRR analysis	Criteria: (1) Highest B/C ratio (2) Highest IRR
2	The results (or the ranking of the alternatives) obtained from these four methods are consistent.	The results (or the ranking of the alternatives) obtained from these two methods are consistent.
3	If $B_1 = B_2 = ... = B_i = ... = B_N$ and $C_1 \neq C_2 \neq ... \neq C_i \neq ... \neq C_N$ (B_i = benefit of Alt i, Ci = cost of Alt i) then, all the six methods contained in both sets are consistent with one another and give the same ranking.	(such as Examples 2.3, 2.4 and 2.8)
4	If $B_1 \neq B_2 \neq ... \neq B_i \neq ... \neq B_N$ and $C_1 = C_2 = ... = C_i = ... = C_N$ then, all the six methods contained in both sets are consistent with one another and give the same ranking.	(such as Examples 3.2 and Problem 2 of Chapter 3)
5	If $B_1 \neq B_2 \neq ... \neq B_i \neq ... \neq B_N$ and $C_1 \neq C_2 \neq ... \neq C_i \neq ... \neq C_N$ then, the conclusion drawn from the methods in the 1st set may not necessarily be consistent with that drawn from the 2nd set.	(such as Example 5.1)

From the summary, it can be seen that the direct B/C ratio and the direct IRR methods (the 2nd set) may arrive at different conclusions when compared to the other methods, viz. the net annual benefit method, the net present worth method, the incremental benefit-cost ratio method and the incremental IRR method (the first set). The readers may now raise such a question: "If inconsistent results were obtained from different methods, which one should be used?" The answer is that in the *economic* appraisal of projects, the methods of the 1st set should be used. The B/C ratio and the. IRR are *financial* indicators of projects only. The discussion in the next section will show that the financial indicators may lead to wrong conclusions in the *economic* comparison of multiple alternatives.

5.5 Variable IRR (Financial Indicator) and Constant NPW (Economic Indicator)

Let us take a look at an all equity case (i.e. initial investment to be supplied wholly by the investor) where an initial investment of $10,000 leads to a receipt of $5,000 each year for the following three years as shown in Table 5.5.1:

Table 5.5.1 Cash flows with $10,000 as equity

End of Year	Cash out	Cash in
0	10,000	
1		5,000
2		5,000
3		5,000

The IRR of this investment is 23.4%.

However, if the investor has $4,000 as equity and borrows $6,000 from a source paying an interest of 10% p.a. for it so that a total of $10,000 initial capital is obtained, the net receipts in the next 3 years, having deducted the amortization and the interest payment from the gross receipt, are calculated to be $2,400, $2,600 and $2,800, as shown in Table 5.5.2.

In other words, the investor will obtain $2,400, $2,600 and $2,800 in year 1, 2 and 3 respectively if he initially invests $4,000. The cash flows of the investment become those as shown in Table 5.5.3. The reader should note that the cash flows in Table 5.5.1 and those in Table 5.5.3 have no advantage over one another as far as the *economic value* of the investment is concerned.

Table 5.5.2 Uniform principal amortization for loan $6,000

End of year	Amount borrowed	Principal amortization	Balance unamortized	Interest (10%)	Total annual payment	Net annual receipt
0	6,000		6,000			
1		2,000	4,000	600	2,600	5,000 – 2,600 = 2,400
2		2,000	2,000	400	2,400	5,000 – 2,400 = 2,600
3		2,000	0	200	2,200	5,000 – 2,200 = 2,800

Table 5.5.3 Cash flows with $4,000 as equity and $6,000 as loan

End of year	Cash out	Cash in
0	4,000	
1		2,400
2		2,600
3		2,800

The IRR is calculated to be 41.2%.

The results are that the IRR of the cash flows shown in Table 5.5.1 is 23.4% and that shown in Table 5.5.3 is 41.2%. According to the highest IRR criterion, the latter case is better than the former case.

However, since the two sets of cash flows in fact have no economic advantage one over another, as already explained a little earlier, the highest IRR criterion in this case leads to a wrong conclusion.

Let us look at a further case. If the investor uses only $1,000 as equity and borrows $9,000 at 10% per annum interest, his annual net receipts in the next 3 years, after deducting annual amortization and interest payment, will be $1,100, $1,400 and $1,700 as shown in Table 5.5.4.

The IRR is calculated to be 113.1 %, which is again different from those which have been previously calculated.

Table 5.5.4 Cash flows with $1,000 as equity and $9,000 as loan

End of Year	Cash out	Cash in
0	1,000	
1		1,100
2		1,400
3		1,700

It can be seen that IRR becomes higher if a bigger loan is made, although the economic value of the investment remains the same in all the three situations. The pressure point is the interest rate of 10% , which is smaller than the IRR of the all-equity case, 23.4%. If the interest rate is not 10% but higher than 23.4%, then an exactly opposite effect will occur, that is, the higher the loan, the lower the IRR that will be obtained. Readers should verify this themselves.

However, if we use the net present worth method to compare the alternatives, the NPWs obtained from the 3 sets of cash flows will be the same, that is, equal to $2,434.26 in all cases if a discount rate of 10% is used:

NPW of cash flows in Table 5.4.1

$$= -10,000 + \frac{5,000}{(1+0.1)} + \frac{5,000}{(1+0.1)^2} + \frac{5,000}{(1+0.1)^3} = 2,434.26$$

NPW of cash flows in Table 5.4.3

$$= -4,000 + \frac{2,400}{(1+0.1)} + \frac{2,600}{(1+0.1)^2} + \frac{2,800}{(1+0.1)^3} = 2,434.26$$

NPW of cash flows in Table 5.4.4

$$= -1,000 + \frac{1,100}{(1+0.1)} + \frac{1,400}{(1+0.1)^2} + \frac{1,700}{(1+0.1)^3} = 2,434.26$$

The NPW is not affected and is constant in all situations. From society's point of view, NPW is a good economic indicator for projects. The IRR is only suitable for use as a *financial* indicator from the private investor's point of view. The NPW (and net annual benefit too) can reflect the real *economic value* of an individual alternative. As far as society's view point is concerned, the highest economic value obtainable is always the criterion for selection of alternatives. From a private investor's point of view, however, the criterion may be different. Assuming the limited availability of money for investment (as a private investor always does), the highest *rate of return* (e.g. IRR which vary as the amount of loan and/or the interest rate vary) will usually be the criterion for private investment decisions.

In conclusion, in the economic appraisal (not financial) of projects, the best way for selecting alternatives is to use the NPW method or the incremental analysis. The direct IRR or B/C method may lead to wrong decisions. Moreover, if the IRR of an investment is ever used to reflect the economic viability, it must be calculated on the basis of the cash flows of an all-equity case (i.e. without loan).

Readers were asked just a little while ago to verify that if the interest rate on loan is higher than 23.4%, it would no longer be advantageous to borrow money, unlike the examples shown in Table 5.5.3 and Table 5.5.4. This phenomenon can be seen from Fig. 5.2 as follows:

The NPW vs. *i* curve shown above has an IRR of 23.4%, which is drawn based on an all-equity cash flow (–$10,000, $5,000, $5,000, $5,000). The other two cash flows with different equity-loan ratios, (–$4,000, $2,400, $2,600, $2,800) and (–$1,000, $1,100, $1,400, $1,700), are derived based on the all-equity cash flow (–$10,000, $5,000, $5,000, $5,000) with an interest rate on loan = 10%. All these three cash flows (one all-equity case and two

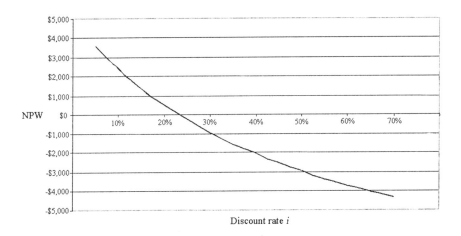

Fig. 5.2 NPW vs. discount rate i.

non-all-equity cases) must have a NPW of $2,434.26, because the NPW of
the all-equity cash flow at $i = 10\%$ is $2,434.26 (see Fig. 5.2). A
mathematical proof for this will be given in Section 5.6. So, any other cash
flows (besides the above three) with different equity-loan ratio derived based
on the all-equity cash flow (–$10,000, $5,000, $5,000, $5,000) with an
interest rate of 10% on loan will also have a NPW of $2,434.26. Similarly,
any other cash flows with different equity-loan ratios derived from the same
all-equity cash flow with an interest rate on loan = 20% will have a NPW of
$532.41 (see Fig. 5.2 also). Furthermore, since the all-equity cash flow has
an IRR = 23.4%, the NPW of it and of all other cash flows with different
equity-loan ratios derived from it based on an loan interest rate of 23.4%
must be also equal to zero. Using the same argument, any cash flows with
different equity-loan ratios derived from the same all-equity cash flow of (–
$10,000, $5,000, $5,000, $5,000) with an interest rate on loan greater than
23.4% will have a negative NPW. Hence, if one borrows money at an
interest rate higher than 23.4% for the investment, he will be in a
disadvantageous position, and vice versa.

5.6 Mathematical Proof for Section 5.5

The example illustrated above that NPW is a constant value in all situations
can be proved mathematically. This section describes the proof. Mathematical induction will be used in the proof.

If we assume that:

C = all-equity case initial capital outlay,
I_i = all-equity case cash-in in year i,
B = loan amount,
A_i = principal amortization in year i,
R = $1 + i$ (i = borrowing interest rate, % per period), and
n = total number of periods.

then, from Table 5.5.2, we can derive that the net annual receipts (cash-in in Table 5.5.3) are as follows:

Cash-in in Yr 1 = $I_1 - (A_1 + BR - B)$
Cash-in in Yr 2 = $I_2 - [A_2 + (B - A_1)R - (B - A_1)]$
Cash-in in Yr 3 = $I_3 - \{A_3 + [B - (A_1 + A_2)]R - [B - (A_1 + A_2)]\}$

$$\vdots$$

Cash-in in Yr n = $I_n - \{A_n + [B - (A_1 + \dots + A_{n-1})]R - [B - (A_1 + \dots + A_{n-1})]\}$

Now, we use mathematical induction to prove that:

$$\frac{I_1 - (A_1 + BR - B)}{R} + \frac{I_2 - [A_2 + (B - A_1)R - (B - A_1)]}{R^2}$$

$$+ \frac{I_3 - \{A_3 + [B - (A_1 + A_2)]R - [B - (A_1 + A_2)]\}}{R^3} + \dots$$

$$+ \frac{I_n - \{A_n + [B - (A_1 + A_2 + \dots + A_{n-1})]R - [B - (A_1 + A_2 + \dots + A_{n-1})]\}}{R^n}$$

$$= \frac{(I_1 R^{n-1} + I_2 R^{n-2} + \dots + I_n) - [(A_1 + A_2 + \dots + A_n) + BR^n - B]}{R^n}$$

Firstly, we must prove that the mathematical expression is true when $n = 2$.

When $n = 2$,

$$\text{LHS} = \frac{I_1 - (A_1 + BR - B)}{R} + \frac{I_2 - [A_2 + (B - A_1)R - (B - A_1)]}{R^2}$$

$$= \frac{I_1 R - A_1 R - BR^2 + BR + I_2 - A_2 - BR + A_1 R - B - A_1}{R^2}$$

$$= \frac{(I_1 R + I_2) - [(A_1 + A_2) + BR^2 - B]}{R^2}$$

$$= \text{RHS}$$

So, the mathematical expression is true when $n = 2$.

Next, we must also prove that if the mathematical expression is true when $n = k$, then it will also be true when $n = k + 1$.

When $n = k + 1$,

$$
\begin{aligned}
\text{LHS} =\ & \frac{I_1 - (A_1 + BR - B)}{R} + \frac{I_2 - [A_2 + (B - A_1)R - (B - A_1)]}{R^2} + \ldots \\
& + \frac{I_k - \{A_k + [B - (A_1 + \ldots + A_{k-1})]R - [B - (A_1 + \ldots + A_{k-1})]\}}{R^k} \\
& + \frac{I_{k+1} - \{A_{k+1} + [B - (A_1 + \ldots + A_k)]R - [B - (A_1 + \ldots + A_k)]\}}{R^{k+1}} \\
=\ & \frac{(I_1 R^{k-1} + I_2 R^{k-2} + \ldots + I_k) - (A_1 + A_2 + \ldots + A_k) + BR^k - B}{R^k} \\
& + \frac{I_{k+1} - \{A_{k+1} + [B - (A_1 + \ldots + A_k)]R - [B - (A_1 + \ldots + A_k)]\}}{R^{k+1}} \quad \text{(since} \\
& \text{it is true for } n = k) \\
=\ & \frac{I_1 R^k + \ldots + I_k R - A_1 R - \ldots - A_k R - BR^{k+1} + BR + I_{k+1} - A_{k+1} - BR}{R^{k+1}} \\
& + \frac{A_1 R + \ldots + A_k R + B - A_1 - \ldots - A_k}{R^{k+1}} \\
=\ & \frac{(I_1 R^k + I_2 R^{k-1} + \ldots + I_{k+1}) - (A_1 + A_2 + \ldots + A_{k+1}) + BR^{k+1} - B}{R^{k+1}} \\
=\ & \text{RHS}
\end{aligned}
$$

Therefore, the mathematical expression is true.

Now, let us go back to look at the calculation of NPW of the cash flows shown in Tables 5.5.3 or 5.5.4. The calculation of the NPW can be generalized as follows:

$$
\begin{aligned}
\text{NPW} \\
=\ & -(C - B) + \frac{I_1 - (A_1 + BR - B)}{R} + \frac{I_2 - [A_2 + (B - A_1)R - (B - A_1)]}{R^2} + \ldots \\
& + \frac{I_n - \{A_n + [B - (A_1 + A_2 + \ldots + A_{n-1})]R - [B - (A_1 + A_2 + \ldots + A_{n-1})]\}}{R^n} \\
=\ & -(C - B) + \frac{(I_1 R^{n-1} + I_2 R^{n-2} + \ldots + I_n) - [(A_1 + A_2 + \ldots + A_n) + BR^n - B]}{R^n}
\end{aligned}
$$

$$= -(C-B) + \frac{(I_1 R^{n-1} + I_2 R^{n-2} + ... + I_n) - (B + BR^n - B)}{R^n}$$

$$= -C + \frac{(I_1 R^{n-1} + I_2 R^{n-2} + ... + I_n)}{R^n}$$

$$= -C + \frac{I_1}{(1+i)} + \frac{I_2}{(1+i)^2} + ... + \frac{I_n}{(1+i)^n}$$

which is the original definition of NPW.

We can see that NPW is independent of B (i.e., the amount of loan) and is only dependent of the all-equity initial capital outlay C and the all-equity cash-in I_i. Hence, the NPW is a constant value since i (the borrowing interest rate) is assumed fixed in this mathematical proof.

It should be noted from the mathematical proof that the NPW is constant regardless of the time length of the amortizations and the amount of amortization in each period. In other words, the amortizations need not be the same every time and the number of amortizations need not equal to n, as long as the sum of all amortizations equals the amount of original loan (i.e. B).

The above illustrative example in Section 5.5 and the mathematical proof in Section 5.6 have been published in the article, "The Variable Financial Indicator IRR and the Constant Economic Indicator NPV", by S. L. Tang and H. John Tang, in *The Engineering Economist*, Vol. 48, No. 1 (2003).

5.7 Conclusion

We have seen in Sections 5.5 and 5.6 that the NPW of a capital investment is constant in all situations and is not affected by the variation of financial arrangements. From a society's point of view, NPW is a good *economic indicator* for projects, as the economic value of an investment does not change even if its financial arrangement changes. The IRR, however, is suitable for use as a *financial indicator* from a private investor's point of view, since private investors usually like to play around with financial arrangements to optimize the rate of return.

As far as the society's viewpoint is concerned, the criterion of the highest economic value (or the highest NPW), the value of which is not affected by differences of financial arrangements, should be the basis for the selection of capital investment alternatives. From the private investor's viewpoint, however, the criterion may be different. Under the circumstances of limited availability of funds, the highest IRR should be a suitable criterion for private investment decisions. The IRR varies as the financial arrangement varies.

As is seen above, the NPW functions as an economic indicator while the IRR functions as a financial indicator. If the IRR of an investment is ever used to reflect the economic viability, it must be calculated on the basis of the cash flows of an all-equity case (i.e. without loan). The evaluation of Financial-IRR (FIRR) and Economic-IRR (EIRR) can be found in Chapter 8. It should be noted that there is only one EIRR (a constant value) but there are different FIRRs for a single capital investment under different financial arrangements. This fact is consistent with the theory that the readers have read in this chapter.

5.8 Problems

1.   There are six alternative ways to improve a production line. The capital costs needed, the extra annual OMR costs required and the extra annual benefits generated from the improvement are as follows:

	Alternatives					
	(1)	(2)	(3)	(4)	(5)	(6)
Capital cost of improvement	150,000	170,000	200,000	350,000	500,000	650,000
Extra annual OMR costs needed	10,000	12,000	15,000	25,000	40,000	50,000
Extra annual benefit generated	41,800	46,500	56,000	93,000	132,000	160,500

Assuming the life of the project to be 10 years and the discount rate to be 12% p.a., find the alternative which gives:
(a)   the highest net annual benefit,
(b)   the highest net present worth,
(c)   the highest direct B/C ratio,
(d)   the highest direct IRR.

Use the following methods to find the best alternative:
(e)   the incremental benefit-cost ratio method,
(f)   the incremental IRR method.

2.   There are two sets of methods in comparing multiple alternatives. They are:

1st set of methods	*2nd set of methods*
(i) Highest net present worth method method	(i) Highest direct B/C *ratio*
(ii) Highest net annual benefit method method	(ii) Highest direct IRR
(iii) Incremental benefit cost ratio method	
(iv) Incremental IRR method	

(a) Are the *methods within each set* consistent with one another in the comparison of multiple alternatives?

(b) Are the *two sets* consistent with each other in the comparison of multiple alternatives? Give examples.

(c) Which set is a better indicator for the *economic* appraisal of projects?

6. Financial versus Economic Appraisals

Let us take an example of a man putting money in a bank. The man obtains interest for the money he deposits. However, in addition to this simple fact, there results a series of activities in the community where he lives. The bank uses the money to give loans to industrialists who in turn use the money to invest in further business and so on. The community may benefit from the repeated utilization of the money in the form of increased employment, increased utilization of resources, increased output and so on. The man can be viewed as an analogy for a private investor/company, and the community as a society/nation. Just as the man is only interested in knowing how much interest he is going to get from the bank, so the private investor is only interested in the *financial* profitability of an investment. However, some financially profitable projects may have good as well as bad effects on the society which cannot be reflected at the level of financial analysis. Such external effects should be dealt with in the economic analysis (some people call this a "socio-economic analysis" or "social profitability analysis"; some even use the term "cost-benefit analysis" — readers should differentiate the last term from benefit-cost ratio). In short, a financial appraisal gives the private investor's point of view, and the economic appraisal gives the society's point of view. Sometimes, a financially viable project may not be economically feasible, and vice versa. In the following section, the financial analysis will be fully discussed. The economic analysis will be discussed in the later part of this chapter.

6.1 Financial Appraisal

The tools used for financial appraisal are those which have been described in Chapters 2 and 3. Out of these several tools, the DCF/IRR method is most commonly adopted. In a financial appraisal, the following two items are tax deductible:
(i)   depreciation of assets,
(ii) interest on loan.

In an all-equity case, there is no loan and therefore no interest has to be paid so only depreciation is tax deductible. In the following two examples, the first one is an all-equity investment and the second one a non-all-equity investment.

Example 6.1

A company is considering setting up a new production line. To do so, a new piece of equipment, which has a life of 4 years and costs $800,000 has to be purchased. The revenue generated is estimated to be $408,000 per annum. The total expenses associated with this production line are estimated to be $100,000 per annum. The profit tax rate is 25%. Assuming a straight-line depreciation for the equipment and ignoring salvage value, carry out a financial analysis for the company.

Solution 6.1

The depreciation of the equipment is assumed to be straight-line (see Appendix 2) so the annual depreciation is $200,000. The revenue, the total cost, the profit before tax and the profit after tax are shown in Table 6.1.

Table 6.1 Income statement for financial analysis

	Year 1	Year 2	Year 3	Year 4
Revenue:	408,000	408,000	408,000	408,000
Cost: Depreciation	200,000	200,000	200,000	200,000
Other expenses	100,000	100,000	100,000	100,000
Total	300,000	300,000	300,000	300,000
Profit before tax	108,000	108,000	108,000	108,000
Tax (25%)	27,000	27,000	27,000	27,000
Profit after tax	81,000	81,000	81,000	81,000

Table 6.1 represents the income statement of the proposed project. The income of $81,000 per annum (i.e. profit after tax) shown in this statement, however, cannot be used to compute the IRR without adjustment. As explained in Section 3.4 of Chapter 3 (Example 3.3 in particular), depreciation must be added to the profit after tax to avoid double counting so that the cash flows obtained are suitable for IRR computation. This is shown in Table 6.2.

Table 6.2 Income statement and cash flow forecast for financial analysis

	Year 1	Year 2	Year 3	Year 4
Revenue	408,000	408,000	408,000	408,000
Cost: Depreciation	200,000	200,000	200,000	200,000
Other expenses	100,000	100,000	100,000	100,000
Total	300,000	300,000	300,000	300,000
Profit before tax	108,000	108,000	108,000	108,000
Tax (25%)	27,000	27,000	27,000	27,000
Profit after tax	81,000	81,000	81,000	81,000
Add depreciation	200,000	200,000	200,000	200,000
Cash flow	281,000	281,000	281,000	281,000

The cash flows shown in Table 6.2 can be used to calculate the IRR of the investment. The reader should note that depreciation is deducted as cost in the first place because it is tax exemptible. After the amount of tax is calculated, depreciation is then added back in order to avoid double counting in the evaluation of IRR. The cash flows can now be represented as:

Table 6.3 Cash flow table for IRR calculation

End of Year	Cash out	Cash in
0	800,000	
1		281,000
2		281,000
3		281,000
4		281,000

In Example 6.1, it is assumed that the entire capital (i.e. equipment cost of $800,000) is supplied by the investor. If he only provides a capital of $200,000 (equity) and borrows the other $600,000 (loan) from a bank at an interest rate of 10% per annum for a period of 3 years to start the new production line, then the financial analysis has to be modified. It will be shown in the following example.

Example 6.2

Repeat doing Example 6.1 if the total capital of $800,000 is made up of $200,000 equity and $600,000 loan, with three equal principal amortizations at the end of years 1, 2 and 3.

Solution 6.2

As mentioned at the beginning of this section, both depreciation and interest on loan are tax deductible. Since loan is involved in this case, the amount of interest payment each year should be known before cash flows can be calculated.

Since the loan is to be amortized in 3 equal installments, that is, $200,000 each year, the interest payment can be calculated using the method as described in Section 1.5 of Chapter 1 and is shown as follows:

End of year	Principal borrowed	Principal amortization	Balance unamortized	Interest (10%)
0	600,000		600,000	
1		200,000	400,000	60,000
2		200,000	200,000	40,000
3		200,000	0	20,000

The interest payment is now known. The next step is to establish the income statement from which the cash flows can be calculated. This is shown in Table 6.4.

As with Example 6.1, the cash flows can be represented as shown in Table 6.5 for computing IRR.

The IRR is now 27%, which is quite a lot greater than 15% as calculated in Example 6.1 (the all-equity case). This is because the all-equity IRR is greater than the interest rate on the loan (10% in this example), as explained very clearly in Section 5.5 of Chapter 5. The reader can also verify that the NPWs of the cash flows of Tables 6.3 and 6.5 remain stable using 10% as the discount rate, although the IRR has changed appreciably. The higher the loan the investor makes, the higher the IRR he will obtain. The NPW, however, will remain stable.

The minimum desirable rate of return can be assumed to be 10% in this situation, because the rate of return of the investment should be at least equal to or greater than the interest rate for the bank loan. In the above financial analysis, the company should invest in the new production line which has a rate of return of 15%. If he can obtain a loan from the bank, he should obtain as high a loan as possible. The analysis shows that if he obtains a loan of $600,000 at 10% interest rate, the rate of return of the investment will increase from 15% to 27%.

Table 6.4 Income statement and cash flow forecast
($200,000 as equity and $600,000 as loan)

	Year 1	Year 2	Year 3	Year 4
Revenue	408,000	408,000	408,000	408,000
Cost: Depreciation	200,000	200,000	200,000	200,000
Other expenses	100,000	100,000	100,000	100,000
Total	300,000	300,000	300,000	300,000
Gross Profit	108,000	108,000	108,000	108,000
Interest payment	60,000	40,000	20,000	0
Profit before tax	48,000	68,000	88,000	108,000
Tax (25%)	12,000	17,000	22,000	27,000
Profit after tax	36,000	51,000	66,000	81,000
Add depreciation	200,000	200,000	200,000	200,000
Cash flow before amortization	236,000	251,000	266,000	281,000
Amortization	200,000	200,000	200,000	0
Cash flow after amortization	36,000	51,000	66,000	281,000

Table 6.5 Cash flow table ($200,000 as equity and $600,000 as loan)

End of Year	Cash out	Cash in
0	200,000	
1		36,000
2		51,000
3		66,000
4		281,000

A remark to Table 6.4 is given by the author as follows. The revenues and costs (rows 1 and 3) in the 4 years are *constant base year prices* (see Section 4.3 of Chapter 4). The interest payments and the principal amortizations (rows 6 and 12), however, are *actual transactions* and are *not* constant year based. So, in this table, the figures are a mixture of real and apparent values. The IRR calculated (i.e. 27%) therefore is not entirely real. The 27% IRR, however, is on a safe side from an investor's point of view. The real IRR should be even higher than 27%. If one desires to have a more accurate real IRR, then the interest payments and the principal amortizations should be adjusted to some lower values by multiplying them with $(pwf)^{n,i}$ with $i = f$, where f is the average inflation rate over the 4 years. Such an exercise is left to the readers.

A case study on financial analysis will be given in Chapter 7, but before that, let us look at what economic analysis is and how it is different from financial analysis.

6.2 Economic Appraisal

In a financial analysis, market prices are always used to represent benefits and costs. For economic analysis in the more advanced countries, it is assumed that the price mechanism works and therefore market prices are also used in the analysis. However, for economic analysis in developing countries, market prices sometimes fail to reflect real costs of inputs to society and real benefits of the outputs attributable to the project. The market imperfection will require adjustment of market prices by converting them into shadow prices, and the latter will be used to represent benefits and costs in the analysis. The conversion is called *shadow pricing* which requires discussion at some length and will be treated in Section 6.4 of this chapter.

Tax payments (income tax, customs duty/tarriffs, etc.) are actual costs to an investor and therefore must be considered in the financial analysis. They are, however, not considered in the economic analysis. This is because they are merely *internal transfers* within a society and there is neither loss nor gain as far as the national standpoint is concerned. To make this simple, let us consider an analogy. A father has three adult sons and all of them are gamblers. The father is gambling with his sons John and Peter. John and Peter are gambling with their brother James. Although there are win and loss for the individuals, there is no win or loss within the family. This same thing happens in society. Although the investor pays tax to the government, the money paid only represents internal transfers within society. It results in no net increase of economic value to the latter. Hence, taxes should be excluded when carrying out an economic analysis.

Consider Example 6.1 and Table 6.2 again. Since tax payment should not be considered, Table 6.2 would become Table 6.6 as shown below.

Readers may find the above calculation a bit tedious because depreciation was deducted first and added later. This observation is exactly right, and in fact, it is not necessary to do so. Example 3.3 of Chapter 3 has already illustrated this point. One can simply write down the cash flows (without going through steps in Table 6.6) as shown in Table 6.7. The reason for deducting and then adding depreciation is that depreciation is tax exemptible and tax payment is considered as a cost in a financial analysis whilst in an economic analysis, such a procedure is not necessary.

If a part of the capital is borrowed for an investment, interest must be paid for the loan borrowed. Interest payment on a loan, like tax payment, is not considered in economic analysis. It has significance only financially but not economically. As explained in the last part of Chapter 5 and particularly at the end of that chapter, the amount of money borrowed for an investment and the interest paid for the loan will only be significant in the financial profitability but will not have the effect of changing the economic value of the investment. All interest payments should be disregarded and the *economic-IRR* (EIRR), the IRR of an economic analysis, should be calculated as if the investment is an all-equity one.

Table 6.6 Income statement and cash flow forecast for economic analysis

	Year 1	Year 2	Year 3	Year 4
Revenue	408,000	408,000	408,000	408,000
Cost: Depreciation	200,000	200,000	200,000	200,000
Other expenses	100,000	100,000	100,000	100,000
Total	300,000	300,000	300,000	300,000
Profit	108,000	108,000	108,000	108,000
Add depreciation	200,000	200,000	200,000	200,000
Cash flow	308,000	308,000	308,000	308,000

Table 6.7 Cash flow table for economic analysis

End of Year	Cash out	Cash in	NCF
0	800,000		−800,000
1	100,000	408,000	308,000
2	100,000	408,000	308,000
3	100,000	408,000	308,000
4	100,000	408,000	308,000

6.3 Identification of Benefits and Costs in Economic Analysis

In the previous section, readers have seen that tax and interest are considered as income transfers and not a cost nor a benefit, and therefore they must be excluded in an economic analysis. The question now is: what should be classified as benefits or costs? The answer is not too difficult: anything that results in an increase of output/national income will be of primary importance. Although income transfers provide the society with the opportunity of fairer distribution, it is only of secondary importance to the problem, particularly in developing countries. The primary concern is, however, whether or not the investment will generate wealth for the society.

To identify and test if anything has primary economic significance, one must ask oneself three questions: (1) if there is any effect on real output which is produced or is destroyed; (2) is there any effect on resource which is utilized or caused to lie idle; (3) is there any effect on saving or increase of consumption? Tax and interest are those things which have no effects and therefore cannot pass the tests, hence they must not be considered. An example of social benefits and social costs identification is given in Example 6.3.

After the social benefits and social costs are identified and tested using the above criteria, they (but not the intangibles) are usually obtained as market prices first and then converted to shadow prices. Shadow prices, as mentioned at the beginning of Section 6.2, are adjustments to market imperfections, and will be further discussed in the next section.

6.4 Shadow Pricing and Opportunity Cost

Shadow pricing is a large topic and its understanding requires profound knowledge of economics. In this section, only an introduction to the basic concepts of shadow pricing will be given. Readers may refer to the World Bank's publication *Economic Analysis of Projects* (by Squire and Van der Tak) if they wish to pursue on the topic.

6.4.1 Market imperfection and shadow factor

If a government exercises import controls, a distortion between the market price and the real cost (i.e. the economic value) of the imported goods will be created. This is an example of market imperfection. If the import control is in the form of customs duty/tariff, then the price before tax, that is, the CIF value (i.e. cost, insurance and freight value) should be used. This is consistent with the discussion in Section 6.2.

Price control policy can also disturb actual prices. For example, if the government enforces a minimum wage law on the employment of labourers (i.e. price control on labour), then the labour cost component of the total project costs will not reflect the true economic value of labourers in the situation. If there is serious unemployment in a society and one of the society's objectives is to create employment, then a shadow price of 0.5 (or zero in very serious case) of the market wage (market wage is the wage paid under minimum wage law) will be used in the economic analysis. In other words, if the wage paid for an unskilled labourer is $50 a day, only $25 a day will be taken as the social cost of the labourer (or even no cost in very serious case). The factor 0.5 (or zero) is called the shadow factor. (Readers are reminded at this juncture that $50 a day of labourer cost must be used in the financial analysis as it represents actual cost to the investor). The shadow price can therefore be expressed as:

Shadow price = market price × shadow factor

Techniques have been developed for deriving shadow factors but the details are outside the scope of this book. Readers who want to know the techniques may refer to the World Bank publication previously mentioned. Normally, these shadow factors are available from the national planning authority of a government.

6.4.2 Opportunity cost

Readers have seen that the shadow price of labour can be valued as zero in case of serious unemployment even though market wages are paid. This is because it costs society nothing to have the unemployed labour utilized. In other words, a labourer does not cause any loss of output from another job opportunity if he is employed in a new job. This is economically beneficial to society because it generates output (see Section 6.3) by employing him without losing output elsewhere, hence resulting an incremental increase of output in the society. However, if he is not unemployed in the first place (assuming there is a shortage of labour in the society), he will have to cease to undertake his existing job in order to have the opportunity of undertaking this particular job. To cease being involved with another job is a cost to the society because it represents a decrease of output elsewhere although an increase of output here compensates for it. The decrease in output (or marginal output) of the labourer, forgone elsewhere because of its use here, is called the opportunity cost. When unemployment prevails in a society, the opportunity cost of labour is zero because an addition of extra labour will not cause any incremental output. However, if there is a shortage of labour in a society, *the willingness to pay* for the cost which will result from the incremental output due to the availability of an extra labourer reflects the economic value of the labour. Therefore, opportunity cost can be referred to as true economic value, as is the shadow price, in an economic analysis.

6.4.3 Price of foreign exchange

The official exchange rate (OER) is fixed by the government. Overvaluation of the country's currency may occur, resulting in a distortion in domestic prices relative to world prices. For example, in the case of serious import controls, the official exchange rate usually understates the value of additional foreign exchange earnings to the economy. This will result in the shadow exchange rate (SER) of local currency per unit of foreign currency being higher than the official exchange rate. The shadow exchange rate can be reflected in the currency exchange in the black market. In the event of trade liberalization (i.e. removing import controls), the shadow and official exchange rates will tend to be the same. In economic analysis, shadow exchange rate should be used instead of official exchange rate.

The above is a very brief account of shadow pricing. Examples of applying shadow pricing will be given in Chapter 8. Readers may be able to understand its concepts and application better when they go through a case study in economic analysis in that chapter.

Example 6.3

There is an existing old and poor single-two road running between Town A and Town B as shown in Fig. 6.1. There is a proposal to construct a new highway to relieve the increasing traffic on the road. After considering all constraints, a new route has been drawn up for constructing the highway to connect the two towns. Identify the social benefits and social costs of the proposed highway project.

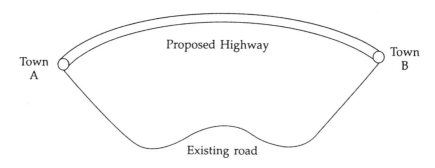

Fig. 6.1 Proposed highway

Solution 6.3

The social benefits and costs identified must be able to pass the tests described in Section 6.3. They are listed in Tables 6.8 and 6.9.

Table 6.8 Social benefits of a highway project

	Social benefits	Remarks
1	Less fuel used by vehicles due to shorter route taken between the two cities and reduced congestion on road.	Saving on consumption of fuel, which is an asset to the society, is a social benefit.
2	Less travelling time taken due to shorter route, bigger road and less congestion.	Saving on travelling time of passengers which means that people (i.e. resources) will not lie idle in the vehicles but will be utilized to do other activities, some of which may generate output.
3	Reduction of maintenance and repair costs to existing road.	Use of society's resources represents an increase in consumption and so is a cost to the society. Maintenance and repair require resources such as labour and material. Reduction of them represents a saving of consumption and is therefore a social benefit. The benefit must be shadowed (see Section 6.4) in the analysis.
4	Fewer injuries to pedestrians.	Injury is a social cost because it causes human resources to lie idle. (The person could have produced output had he or she not been injured.) Reduction of such a social cost is a social benefit.
5	Benefits as a result of greater turn-over in business because of better communication and transportation.	This is not a primary social benefit but a secondary one. To a certain extent it represents transfers/distribution, and therefore is excluded in an economic analysis when the main concern of the society is an efficient economy. However, if the major concern is income distribution, then this "secondary benefit" becomes primary and important.

Table 6.9 Social costs of a highway project

	Social costs	Remarks
1	Costs of resources used in the highway construction.	The resources are mainly labour, material and plant. The costs must be shadowed in the analysis.
2	Maintenance and repair costs to new highway.	See remark of item 3 of social benefit.
3	Loss of crop production due to the fact that the land originally used for cultivation is now used as a highway.	Annual output of crop is destroyed. This is a social cost. This is in fact the land cost in economic analysis.

There are intangible social benefits also such as: the prestige of society due to better infrastructure; the opportunity for development in aspects such as education, recreation, entertainment, commerce and so on due to better transportation; reduction of noise, air and visual pollution to the area along the existing road.

The intangible social costs include the introduction of noise, air and visual pollution, social disruption and danger inflicted on residents around the new highway.

The reader should note that items 1, 2, 4 and 5 listed in Table 6.8 would not be considered in a financial analysis if the highway were to be built by private investors and people were charged for using it. The benefits used in the financial analysis would be the toll paid by vehicles using the highway (see Example 4.3 of Chapter 4). Toll is considered a transfer and so is not included in an economic analysis. Market prices would be used in the financial analysis and tax payments should be included as cost.

6.5 Problems

1. Discuss the difference between a financial analysis and an economic analysis.

2. Explain shadow pricing. Give examples to illustrate your answer.

3. In performing an economic feasibility study of a highway project, what social benefits and costs, both tangible and intangible, could you identify in the study?

Part II

CASE STUDIES

7. Case Study: Financial Feasibility

7.1 The Proposed Project

The project is concerned with the manufacture and sales of an import substitute consumer product. The existing product in the market is totally imported. In order to compete with the existing product, the substitute should have a price advantage over the imported one. The partners of the company conducted a market survey and the following is the result:

Existing supply: All imported
Total annual demand: 400,000 units/year

Proposed annual market share of local product (the proposed project):

Year 1   30% (i.e. 120,000 units)
Year 2   40% (i.e. 160,000 units)
Year 3 to 10   50% (i.e. 200,000 units)

(Proposed maximum capacity of production is 200,000 units/year which will be attained in the 3rd year; the life of the project for financial analysis is assumed to be 10 years).

Price of existing product (imported) to wholesale suppliers = $125/unit.
Proposed price of local product to wholesale suppliers = $100/unit.
Promoting and advertising expenses = $10/unit.

A technical study was also carried out. The method of production was investigated and the cost of production was finalized as follows:

Raw materials   = $20/unit
Labour   = $15/unit
Overheads   = $13/unit
∴ Cost of finished goods = $48/unit

The cost of setting up the plant and the working capital were also found. For estimating the working capital, the following assumptions were made:

Accounts receivable (i.e. the finished
  goods distributed to wholesale
  suppliers who have not yet
  paid for the goods)   = 1 month sales
Inventory:
  Raw materials   = 1 month usage
  Goods-in-process   = 1/2 month of cost of finished goods
  Finished goods   = 1 month of finished goods
Operating expenses
  (company overheads)   = 1 month of operation costs

With the above assumptions, the total capital required was estimated as follows:

1. Plants proper

Plant and equipment, building	= $ 15,000,000
Land	= $ 5,000,000
	$ 20,000,000

2. Working capital

Accounts receivable (1 month)	= $ 1,000,000[1]
Inventory	
Raw materials (1 month)	= $ 200,000[2]
Goods-in-process (1/2 month)	= $ 240,000[3]
Finished goods (1 month)	= $ 480,000[4]
Operation expenses (1 month)	= $ 150,000 (given)
	$ 2,070,000

Total capital required $ 22,070,000

Note:

1. Accounts receivable	= 1 month sales
	= 1st year sales/12
	= ($100/unit × 120,000)/12
	= $1,000,000
2. 1 month raw material cost	= 1st year raw material cost/12
	= ($20/unit × 120,000)/12
	= $200,000
3. 1/2 month of cost of finished goods	= $240,000 (see (4) below)
4. 1 month of finished goods	= 1st year production/12
	= ($48/unit × 120,000)/12
	= $480,000

From the above data, a financial analysis was carried out. Tax rate was assumed to be 25%. A pro-forma income statement (Table 7.1) was prepared. The cash-flow forecast and the calculation of IRR are shown in Tables 7.2 and 7.3 respectively. Readers should revise Example 6.1 of Chapter 6 before going through these three tables.

Table 7.1 Pro-forma income statement (constant base year prices)

	Year	1	2	3–10
1.	Sales	12,000,000	16,000,000	20,000,000
2.	Expenditure			
	Cost of finished goods			
	Raw material	2,400,000	3,200,000	4,000,000
	Labour	1,800,000	2,400,000	3,000,000
	Overheads	1,560,000	2,080,000	2,600,000
	Subtotal	5,760,000	7,680,000	9,600,000
	Depreciation*	1,500,000	1,500,000	1,500,000
	Operating expenses	1,800,000	1,800,000	1,800,000
	Promoting and advertising expenses	1,200,000	1,600,000	2,000,000
	Total expenditure	10,260,000	12,580,000	14,900,000
3.	Profit before tax	1,740,000	3,420,000	5,100,000
4.	Income tax (25%)	435,000	855,000	1,275,000
5.	Profit after tax	1,305,000	2,565,000	3,825,000

* Depreciation (straight-line) for plant proper only (excluding land cost)
= \$15,000,000/10 = \$1,500,000 p.a.

Table 7.2 Cash flow forecast (constant base year prices in thousand dollars)

	Year	1	2	3–10
1.	Income	12,000	16,000	20,000
2.	*Less* expenditure	10,260	12,580	14,900
3.	Profit before tax	1,740	3,420	5,100
4.	Income tax	435	855	1,275
5.	Net income	1,305	2,565	3,825
6.	Add depreciation	1,500	1,500	1,500
7.	Cash flow	2,805	4,065	5,325

Table 7.3 Calculation of IRR (all equity case)

End of year	Cash out ($ × 10³)	Cash in ($ × 10³)	NCF ($ × 10³)	pwf* (18.2%)	DCF ($ × 10³)
0	22,070		−22,070	1	−22,070
1		2,805	2,805	0.846	2,373
2		4,065	4,065	0.716	2,910
3		5,325	5,325	0.606	3,226
4		5,325	5,325	0.513	2,730
5		5,325	5,325	0.434	2,310
6		5,325	5,325	0.367	1,954
7		5,325	5,325	0.311	1,654
8		5,325	5,325	0.263	1,399
9		5,325	5,325	0.222	1,184
10		12,395**	12,395	0.188	2,332
				(approx)	Σ = 0

* IRR = 18.2% is the result of the computer run (Appendix 3)
** Cash-in of year 10 = 10th year cash flow + salvage value
   = 5,325 + (land cost + working capital)
   = 5,325 + (5,000 + 2,070)
   = 12,395

7.2 Sources of Investment Funds

These financial statements were sent to a few equipment suppliers and prospective financial companies from whom the partners hoped to obtain financial assistance.

A foreign equipment supplier and creditor showed interest in financing the proposed project and was willing to supply the building. plant and equipment needs on the following terms:

a. 20% down payment;
b. balance payable in 10 equal annual principal amortizations;
c. interest on the balance of 12% per annum, payable coincident with principal amortizations;
d. secured by a mortgage of plant proper.

A local bank likewise showed interest in the project and was willing to grant up to $10,000,000 under the following conditions:

a.   principal amortizations in 10 equal annual payments;
b.   interest of 12% per annum on outstanding balance payable coincident with principal amortizations;
c.   service charge of 1% per annum on the loan;
d.   secured by a mortgage on plant and equipment.

Another source was a small local financing company who agreed to finance up to 70% of the value of land under the following terms:

a.   payable in 5 equal annual principal installments;
b.   interest of 10% per annum on the outstanding balance payable coincident with principal amortizations;
c.   secured by a mortgage on the land.

The partners had $7,200,000 cash reserved for investing on the project. An additional source of capital was offered by a potential investor who was willing to invest $12,000,000 on the project because he was optimistic about the return of the investment as he thought that the partners' price assumptions were too conservative. The partners were, however, reluctant to accept the offer because it would mean a surrender of control of the project to a single investor.

7.3 The Partners' Decision

In view of the attractive rate of return, the partners decided to go ahead with the project without accepting the offer of the local bank and that of the potential investor. Sources of investment capital were finalized as follows:

Source	Amount
A. Foreign equipment supplier and creditor	$12,000,000 (i.e. $15,000,000 – 20% down payment) for 10 years; $1,200,000 p.a. at 12% interest on the balance.
B. Local financing company	$3,500,000 (i.e. 70% of land cost) for the first 5 years; $700,000 p.a. at 10% interest on the balance.
C. Partners	$ 6,570,000 (< $7,200,000 O.K.)
Total:	$22,070,000

The details of payment for redeeming loans were shown in Table 7.4. The amortizations and interest payments were incorporated in the final income statement (Table 7.5). Readers should note that Items 1 to 3 in this table are similar to those in Table 7.1. The new IRR was then calculated. It was found to be about 27.7% (Table 7.6).

Table 7.4 Loan redemption ($ × 10³)

End of year	Foreign supplier and creditor			Local financing company			Total principal amorti-zation	Total interest payment
	Principal amorti-zation	Balance	Interest (12%)	Principal amorti-zation	Balance	Interest (10%)		
1	1.200	12,000	1,440	700	3,500	350	1,900	1,790
2	1,200	10,800	1,296	700	2,800	200	1,900	1,576
3	1,200	9,600	1,152	700	2,100	210	1,900	1,362
4	1,200	8,400	1,008	700	1,400	140	1,900	1,148
5	1,200	7,200	864	700	700	70	1,900	934
6	1,200	6,000	720				1,200	720
7	1,200	4,800	576				1,200	576
8	1,200	3,600	432				1,200	432
9	1,200	2,400	288				1,200	288
10	1,200	1,200	144				1,200	144

Table 7.5 Final income statement and cash flow forecast (in $ \times 10^3$)

Year	1	2	3	4	5	6	7	8	9	10
1 Sales	12,000	16,000	20,000	20,000	20,000	20,000	20,000	20,000	20,000	20,000
2 Expenditure										
Cost of finished goods										
Raw material	2,400	3,200	4,000	4,000	4,000	4,000	4,000	4,000	4,000	4,000
Labour	1,800	2,400	3,000	3,000	3,000	3,000	3,000	3,000	3,000	3,000
Overheads	1,560	2,080	2,600	2,600	2,600	2,600	2,600	2,600	2,600	2,600
Subtotal	5,760	7,680	9,600	9,600	9,600	9,600	9,600	9,600	9,600	9,600
Depreciation	1,500	1,500	1,500	1,500	1,500	1,500	1,500	1,500	1,500	1,500
Operating expenses	1,800	1,800	1,800	1,800	1,800	1,800	1,800	1,800	1,800	1,800
Promoting and advertising expenses	1,200	1,600	2,000	2,000	2,000	2,000	2,000	2,000	2,000	2,000
Total expenditure	10,260	12,580	14,900	14,900	14,900	14,900	14,900	14,900	14,900	14,900
3 Gross profit	1,740	3,420	5,100	5,100	5,100	5,100	5,100	5,100	5,100	5,100
4 Interest	1,790	1,576	1,362	1,148	934	720	576	432	288	144
5 Taxable income	(50)	1,844	3,738	3,952	4,166	4,380	4,524	4,668	4,812	4,956
6 Tax (25%)	0	461	935	988	1,042	1,095	1,131	1,167	1,203	1,239
7 Profit after tax	(50)	1,333	2,803	2,964	3,124	3,285	3,393	3,501	3,609	3,717
8 *Add* depreciation	1,500	1,500	1,500	1,500	1,500	1,500	1,500	1,500	1,500	1,500
9 *Less* amortization	1,900	1,900	1,900	1,900	1,900	1,200	1,200	1,200	1,200	1,200
10 Cash flow (dividend)	(450)	933	2,403	2,564	2,724	3,585	3,693	3,801	3,909	4,017

Table 7.6 Calculation of IRR ($6,570,000 of equity and $15,500,000 of loan)

End of year	Cash out	Cash in	NCF	$(pwf)^{27.7\%}$	DCF
0	6,570		−6,570	1	−6,570
1	450		−450	0.783	−352
2		933	933	0.613	570
3		2,403	2,403	0.480	1,154
4		2,564	2,564	0.376	964
5		2,724	2,724	0.295	802
6		3,585	3,585	0.231	827
7		3,693	3,693	0.181	667
8		3,801	3,801	0.141	538
9		3,909	3,909	0.111	433
10		11,087*	11,087	0.087	962
				(approx)	$\Sigma = 0$

*Cash in of year 10 = 4,017 + salvage value
= 4,017 + (5,000 + 2,070)
= 11,087

The IRR calculated is 27.7%.

8. Case Study: Economic Feasibility

8.1 Project Brief

A scheme has been drawn up for constructing a new highway to connect two towns (see the diagram in Example 6.3 of Chapter 6) to relieve the increasing and already congested traffic on an existing road connecting the towns. The new highway will be significantly shorter than the existing road. The estimated market price of the construction is $2,200 million and it will take two years to construct. The initial capital outlay is $800 million. The remaining amount has to be invested at $700 million each at the end of year 1 and year 2.

8.2 Relevant Data

Project life assumed   = 25 years

Length of highway   = 36 km

Length of existing road   = 48 km

Capital cost   = $2,200 million
    Preoperation Year 0: $800m
    Preoperation Year 1: $700m
    Preoperation Year 2: $700m

    Material & equipment (imported) = 15%
    Material & equipment (local)   = 35%
    Skilled labour cost   = 10%
    Unskilled labour cost   = 20%
    Overheads   = 20%

Average number of vehicles:
    Buses: 856/day   Lorries: 2,132/day
    Cars: 3,865/day   Motorcycles: 524/day

Cost of travelling time:

Buses	$1,000/hr
Lorries	$ 400/hr
Cars	$ 300/hr
Motorcycles	$ 50/hr

The cost of travelling time is assumed by considering the social status of passengers and the type of goods in lorries.

Operating cost of vehicles:

Buses	$9.0/km
Lorries	$8.0/km
Cars	$5.2/km
Motorcycles	$2.0/km

The operating cost is arrived at by taking into account the cost of fuel, operation charges, wear and tear, etc.

Maintenance cost to road:

Material and equipment (imported)	= 5%
Material and equipment (local)	= 45%
Skilled labour cost	= 10%
Unskilled labour cost	= 20%
Overheads	= 20%

Highway maintenance:
$100,000/km/year in the 1st year;
$200,000/km/year in the 2nd year;
$400,000/km/year in the 3rd year;
$600,000/km/year in the 4th and subsequent years.

Existing road maintenance:
$450,000/km/year before the highway is constructed;
$180,000/km/year after the highway is constructed.

Costs of injuries:
Existing road:

Average number of injuries: Non-fatal cases	= 280/year
Fatal cases	= 12/year
Average wage of the injured	= $200/ day
Average number of days lost in work per injury	= 14
Average compensation to each fatal case	= $360,000

New highway:
Assume 50% fewer injuries in total (both new highway and existing road) after the opening of highway.
Loss of annual crop production (due to the curtailment of cultivated land resulting from highway construction):
Annual crop production = $300,000/ha/year

8.3 Social Benefits

The following social benefits have been quantified:

a. Saving in operating cost (assuming no traffic congestion in both roads) due to shorter distance travelled $ 160.90m   (Table 8.1)

b. Saving in time travelling (assuming no traffic congestion in both roads) $ 253.40m   (Table 8.2)

c. Extra saving in operation cost due to the relief of congestion on the existing road $ 78.40m   (Table 8.3)

d. Extra saving in time of travelling due to the relief of congestion on the existing road $ 103.00m   (Table 8.4)

e. Saving due to reduction of maintenance cost to existing road $ 11.43m   (Table 8.5)

f. Saving on account of fewer injuries $ 1.53m   (Table 8.6)

Total = $ 608.66m

There are other social benefits which have not been quantified (see Example 6.3 of Chapter 6). This does not mean that all those benefits are not quantifiable. Some of them are quantifiable and some are not. Sometimes a social benefit is not quantified because its raw data are too expensive or too difficult to acquire. For those social benefits which are not quantified (and therefore not included in the cost-benefit calculation), they must be thoroughly discussed verbally in the project feasibility report.

8.4 Social Costs

The following social costs have been quantified:

a. Capital costs of construction (shadowed)
    End of Preoperation Year 0 $ 678.00m
    End of Preoperation Year 1 $ 593.25m   } (Table 8.7)
    End of Preoperation Year 2 $ 593.25m

b. Highway maintenance cost (shadowed)
    End of Year 1 $ 3.18m
    End of Year 2 $ 6.35m   } (Table 8.8)
    End of Year 3 $ 12.71m
    End of Year 4 $ 19.06m

c. Loss of annual crop production $ 25.90m   (Table 8.9)

Summary of social costs:

End of year	Capital cost ($m)	Maintenancecost ($m)	Loss of crop ($m)	Total ($m)
Preoperation 0	678			678
Preoperation 1	593.25		25.9	619.15
Preoperation 2	593.25		25.9	619.15
1		3.18	25.9	29.08
2		6.35	25.9	32.25
3		12.71	25.9	38.61
4		19.06	25.9	44.96
5		19.06	25.9	44.96
6		19.06	25.9	44.96
.		.	.	.
.		.	.	.
.		.	.	.
25		19.06	25.9	44.96

As with social benefit, there are other social costs which have not been quantified (see Example 6.3). They should be discussed thoroughly in the project feasibility report.

8.5 Cost-benefit Analysis

The social benefits and social costs have been identified and quantified in Sections 8.3 and 8.4 respectively. The present worth can be calculated based on the figures contained in those two sections. The calculation is shown in Table 8.10. The present worth of the net social benefit is found to be $3,057.56m using a time horizon of 25 years and a discount rate of 10% per annum.

8.6 Sensitivity and Risk Analysis

Sensitivity analysis is concerned with investigating the change of the present worth resulting from a change of certain important parameters (e.g. discount rate, social benefits). What will happen with the present worth if the discount rate is larger or smaller than 10%? Or what will happen if the social benefits turn out to be less than have been estimated? In the following sensitivity analysis, the effects of a change of these two parameters are investigated. Present worth with 6% and 14% discount rates have been calculated, as have those with 80% and 60% of full social benefits. The calculations are shown in Tables 8.11 to 8.18. The results can be sum-marized as follows:

	Full social benefit	80% social benefit	60% social benefit
10% discount rate	3,057.56	2,033.04	1,008.56
14% discount rate	1,611.86	906.33	201.38
6% discount rate	5,712.02	4,110.34	2,508.71

There are 9 figures in the above summary. Some people may like to have more figures with different intervals of the parameters. Sometimes, negative figures may be obtained. The decision maker will decide whether or not to go ahead with the project on the basis of these figures. A risk analysis may be able to help the decision makers which to choose. In a risk analysis, the probability of occurrence on each of the cases will be estimated. Let them be $P_1, P_2, ..., P_9$ ($P_1 + P_2 + ... + P_9 = 1$) as follows:

	Full social benefit	80% social benefit	60% social benefit
10% discount rate	P_1	P_2	P_3
14% discount rate	P_4	P_5	P_6
6% discount rate	P_7	P_8	P_9

The present worth *of* the *expected net social benefit* is the sum of the products of P_i and its corresponding present worth of net social benefit, that is, if $X_1, X_2, ..., X_9$ ($X_1 = 3,057.56$, $X_2 = 2,033.04$, etc.) are the present worth of net social benefits, then

$$\text{Present worth } of \text{ the expected net social benefit} = \sum_{i=1}^{9} P_i X_i$$

The present worth of the expected net social benefit is an important indicator to the decision maker. The above has described a simple but practical form of sensitivity/risk analysis in an economic appraisal.

Table 8.1 Saving in operating cost (Assuming no congestion on existing road)

Vehicles	Difference in distance km	Operating cost/km	Saving in operating cost	Number of vehicles/day	Total saving of operating cost/day
Buses	12	9.0	108.0	856	92,448
Lorries	12	8.0	96.0	2,132	204,672
Cars	12	5.2	62.4	3,865	241,176
Motorcycles	12	2.0	24.0	524	12,576
				Total =	$550,872

Difference in distance = 48 – 36 = 12 km

Total saving of operating cost in a year = $550,872 × 365 = $201m

Assuming 80% of vehicles using the new highway,
actual saving of operating cost = $201 × 80% = $160.9m

Table 8.2 Saving in time travelling (assuming no congestion *on* existing road)

Vehicles	Difference in time to travel (hr)	Cost of travelling time/hr	Number of vehicles/day	Total saving of travelling time/day
Buses	0.5	1,000	856	428,000
Lorries	0.5	400	2,132	426,400
Cilrs	0.5	300	3,865	579,750
Motorcycles	0.5	50	524	13,100
			Total =	$1,447,250

It takes about 0.75 hr to finish travelling on the new highway, but takes about 1.25 hrs to do so on the existing road.

Total saving in time of travelling in 1 year
= $1,447,250 × 365 = $528m

Assuming 40% non-working time saving and 80% of vehicles using the new highway,
actual saving in time = $528 × 60% × 80% = $253.4m

Table 8.3 Extra saving in operating cost (assuming congestion on existing road)

Vehicles	Distance km	Operating cost/km	Operating cost	Number of vehicles/day	Total operating cost/day
Buses	48	9.0	432.0	856	369,792
Lorries	48	8.0	384.0	2,132	818,688
Cars	48	5.2	249.6	3,865	964,704
Motorcycles	48	2.0	96.0	524	50,304
				Total =	$2,203,488

Assuming 15% increase in operating cost is due to congestion,
Total increase of operating cost due to congestion in a year
= $2,203,488 × 365 × 15% = $120.6m

Assuming 65% of the traffic is congested,
actual extra saving in operating cost in a year = $120.6 × 65% = $78.4m

Table 84 Extra saving in travelling time (assuming congestion on existing road)

Vehicles	Extra time (hr)	Cost of travelling time/hr	Number of vehicles/day	Total extra saving/day
Buses	0.25	1,000	856	214,000
Lorries	0.25	400	2,132	213,200
Cars	0.25	300	3,865	289,875
Motorcycles	0.25	50	524	6,550
			Total =	$723,625

It takes 15 hrs to finish travelling on the existing road if there is congestion.

Extra travelling time = 1.5 – 1.25 = 0.25 hr

Total extra time saving in a year (assuming 65% congested traffic)
= $723,625 × 365 × 65%= $171.7m

Assuming 40% non-working time saving,
actual extra time saving in a year = $1717 × 60% = $103m

Table 8.5 Saving in maintenance of existing road

Cost of maintenance on existing road before the construction of highway
= $450,000/km/year × 48km
= $21.6m/year

5% of the total cost is imported material and equipment on which 35% import tax is posed.

Import tax = $21.6 x 5% x 35% = $0.38m

20% of the total cost is unskilled labour on which 50% shadow price is allowed.

Shadowed unskilled labour cost = $21.6 × 20% × 50% = $2.16m

Adjusted total cost in a year = $21.6 – $0.38 – $2.16 = $19.06m

Cost of maintenance on existing road after the construction of the highway
= $180,000/km/year × 48km
= $8.64m/year

Similarly, the adjusted total maintenance cost in a year
= $8.64 – ($8.64 × 5% × 35%) – ($8.64 × 20% × 50%)
= $8.64 – $0.15 – $0.86
= $7.63m

Saving in maintenance of existing road in a year
= $19.06 – $7.63
= $11.43m

Table 8.6 Saving on loss due to injuries

	No. of persons/year	Average wage/day	Average loss in work (days)	Fatal case compensation	Total loss
Non-fatal cases	280	200	14		748,000
Fatal cases	12			360,000	4,320,000
				Total =	$5,104,000

The injured people are categorized as 30% skilled, 60% unskilled and 10% as idle. 50% shadow price is allowed on unskilled labour.

Adjusted loss due to injuries in a year
= ($5,104,000 × 30%) + ($5,104,000 × 60% × 50%)
= $1,531,200 + $1,531,200
= $306m

Saving on losses = $306 × 05 = $153m

Table 8.7 Capital cost of highway construction

Total capital cost = $2,200m

15% of the total cost is imported material and equipment on which 35% import tax is posed.

Import tax = $2,200 × 15% × 35% = $115.5m

20% of the total cost is unskilled labour on which 50% shadow price is allowed.

Shadowed unskilled labour cost = $2,200 × 20% × 50% = $220m

Adjusted total capital cost = $2,200 – $115.5 – $220 = $1,864.5m

Initial capital outlay = $678m

Capital outlay at the end of preoperation year 1 = $593.25m

Capital outlay at the end of preoperation year 2 = $593.25m

Table 8.8 Maintenance cost of new highway

Cost of maintenance on the highway in the first year
= $100,000/km/year × 36km = $3.6m

5% of the total cost is imported material and equipment on which 35% import tax is posed.

Import tax = $3.6 × 5% × 35% = $0.06m

20% of the total cost is unskilled lilbour on which 50% shildow price is allowed.

Shadowed unskilled labour cost = $3.6 × 20% × 50% = $0.36m

Adjusted cost of maintenance in the first year
= $3.6 – $0.06 – $0.36 = $3.18m

Simililrly, maintenance cost in the second year
= $7.2 – ($7.2 × 5% × 35%) – ($7.2 × 20% × 50%)
= $6.35m

Maintenance cost in the third year
= $14.4 – ($14.4 × 5% × 35%) – ($14.4 × 20% × 50%)
= $12.71m

Maintenance cost in the fourth and subsequent years
= $21.6 – ($21.6 × 5% × 35%) – ($21.6 × 20% × 50%)
= $19.06m

Table 8.9 Annual loss of crop production

Length of highway = 36 km

Affected width = 40m

Area of curtailed land = 36,000m × 40m = 144 Ha

Assuming 60% of the curtailed land is cultivated land,
loss of cultivated lilnd = 144 × 60% = 86.4 Ha

Annual loss of crop production = $300,000/Ha × 86.4 = $25.9m

Table 8.10 Calculation of present worth of net social benefit
(full benefit and 10% discount rate)

End of year		Cash out	Cash in*	NCF	$(pwf)^{10\%}$	$(DCF)^{10\%}$
Preoperation	0	678		−678	1	−678
Preoperation	1	619.15		−619.15	0.909	−562.81
Preoperation	2	619.15		−619.15	0.826	−511.42
	1	29.08	608.66	579.58	0.751	435.26
	2	32.25	608.66	576.41	0.683	393.69
	3	38.61	608.66	570.05	0.621	354.00
	4	44.96	608.66	563.70	0.564	317.93
	5	44.96	608.66	563.70	0.513	289.18
	6	44.96	669.53	624.57	0.467	291.67
	7	44.96	669.53	624.57	0.424	264.82
	8	44.96	669.53	624.57	0.386	241.08
	9	44.96	669.53	624.57	0.350	218.60
	10	44.96	669.53	624.57	0.319	199.24
	11	44.96	736.48	691.52	0.290	200.54
	12	44.96	736.48	691.52	0.263	181.87
	13	44.96	736.48	691.52	0.239	165.27
	14	44.96	736.48	691.52	0.218	150.75
	15	44.96	736.48	691.52	0.198	136.92
	16	44.96	810.13	765.17	0.180	137.73
	17	44.96	810.13	765.17	0.164	125.49
	18	44.96	810.13	765.17	0.149	114.01
	19	44.96	810.13	765.17	0.135	103.30
	20	44.96	810.13	765.17	0.123	94.12
	21	44.96	891.14	846.18	0.112	94.77
	22	44.96	891.14	846.18	0.102	86.31
	23	44.96	891.14	846.18	0.092	77.85
	24	44.96	891.14	846.18	0.084	71.08
	25	44.96	891.14	846.18	0.076	64.31
						3,057.56

* Growth rate of vehicles is assumed to be 10% every 5 years. The social benefit is hence increased by 10% in every 5 years.

Table 8.11 Calculation of present worth of net social benefit
(80% benefit and 10% discount rate)

End of year		Cash out	Cash in	NCF	$(pwf)^{10\%}$	$(DCF)^{10\%}$
Preoperation	0	678		−678	1	−678
Preoperation	1	619.15		619.15	0.909	−562.81
Preoperation	2	619.15		619.15	0.826	−511.42
	1	29.08	486.93	457.85	0.751	343.85
	2	32.25	486.93	454.68	0.683	310.55
	3	38.61	486.93	448.32	0.621	278.41
	4	44.96	486.93	441.97	0.564	249.27
	5	44.96	486.93	441.97	0.513	226.73
	6	44.96	535.62	490.66	0.467	229.14
	7	44.96	535.62	490.66	0.424	208.04
	8	44.96	535.62	490.66	0.386	189.39
	9	44.96	535.62	490.66	0.350	171.73
	10	44.96	535.62	490.66	0.319	156.52
	11	44.96	589.18	544.22	0.290	157.82
	12	44.96	589.18	544.22	0.263	143.13
	13	44.96	589.18	544.22	0.239	130.07
	14	44.96	589.18	544.22	0.218	118.64
	15	44.96	589.18	544.22	0.198	107.76
	16	44.96	648.10	603.14	0.180	108.57
	17	44.96	648.10	603.14	0.164	98.91
	18	44.96	648.10	603.14	0.149	89.87
	19	44.96	648.10	603.14	0.135	81.42
	20	44.96	648.10	603.14	0.123	74.19
	21	44.96	712.91	667.95	0.112	74.81
	22	44.96	712.91	667.95	0.102	68.13
	23	44.96	712.91	667.95	0.092	61.45
	24	44.96	712.91	667.95	0.084	56.11
	25	44.96	712.91	667.95	0.076	50.76
						2,033.04

Table 8.12 Calculation of present worth of net social benefit
(60% benefit and 10% discount rate)

End of year		Cash out	Cash in	NCF	$(pwf)^{10\%}$	$(DCF)^{10\%}$
Preoperation	0	678		−678	1	− 678
Preoperation	1	619.15		−619.15	0.909	− 562.81
Preoperation	2	619.15		619.15	0.826	− 511.42
	1	29.08	365.20	336.12	0.751	252.43
	2	32.25	365.20	332.95	0.683	227.40
	3	38.61	365.20	326.59	0.621	202.81
	4	44.96	365.20	320.24	0.564	180.62
	5	44.96	365.20	320.24	0.513	164.28
	6	44.96	401.72	356.76	0.467	166.61
	7	44.96	401.72	356.76	0.424	151.27
	8	44.96	401.72	356.76	0.386	137.71
	9	44.96	401.72	356.76	0.350	124.87
	10	44.96	401.72	356.76	0.319	113.81
	11	44.96	441.89	396.93	0.290	115.11
	12	44.96	441.89	396.93	0.263	104.39
	13	44.96	441.89	396.93	0.239	94.87
	14	44.96	441.89	396.93	0.218	86.53
	15	44.96	441.89	396.93	0.198	78.59
	16	44.96	486.08	441.12	0.180	79.40
	17	44.96	486.08	441.12	0.164	72.34
	18	44.96	486.08	441.12	0.149	65.73
	19	44.96	486.08	441.12	0.135	59.55
	20	44.96	486.08	441.12	0.123	54.26
	21	44.96	534.68	489.72	0.112	54.85
	22	44.96	534.68	489.72	0.102	49.95
	23	44.96	534.68	489.72	0.092	45.05
	24	44.96	534.68	489.72	0.084	41.14
	25	44.96	534.68	489.72	0.076	37.22
						1,008.56

Table 8.13 Calculation of present worth of net social benefit
(full benefit and 14% discount rate)

End of year		Cash out	Cash in	NCF	(pwf)$^{14\%}$	(DCF)$^{14\%}$
Preoperation	0	678		−678	1	−678
Preoperation	1	619.15		−619.15	0.877	−542.99
Preoperation	2	619.15		−619.15	0.769	−476.13
	1	29.08	608.66	579.58	0.675	391.22
	2	32.25	608.66	576.41	0.592	341.23
	3	38.61	608.66	570.05	0.519	295.86
	4	44.96	608.66	563.70	0.456	257.05
	5	44.96	608.66	563.70	0.400	225.48
	6	44.96	669.53	624.57	0.351	219.22
	7	44.96	669.53	624.57	0.308	192.37
	8	44.96	669.53	624.57	0.270	168.63
	9	44.96	669.53	624.57	0.237	148.02
	10	44.96	669.53	624.57	0.208	129.91
	11	44.96	736.48	691.52	0.182	125.86
	12	44.96	736.48	691.52	0.160	110.64
	13	44.96	736.48	691.52	0.140	96.81
	14	44.96	736.48	691.52	0.123	85.06
	15	44.96	736.48	691.52	0.108	74.68
	16	44.96	810.13	765.17	0.095	72.69
	17	44.96	810.13	765.17	0.083	63.51
	18	44.96	810.13	765.17	0.073	55.86
	19	44.96	810.13	765.17	0.064	48.97
	20	44.96	810.13	765.17	0.056	42.85
	21	44.96	891.14	846.18	0.049	41.46
	22	44.96	891.14	846.18	0.043	36.39
	23	44.96	891.14	846.18	0.038	32.15
	24	44.96	891.14	846.18	0.033	28.52
	25	44.96	891.14	846.18	0.029	24.54
						1,611.86

Table 8.14 Calculation of present worth of net social benefit
(80% benefit and 14'% discount rate)

End of year		Cash out	Cash in	NCF	$(pwf)^{14\%}$	$(DCF)^{14\%}$
Preoperation	0	678		−678	1	−678
Preoperation	1	619.15		−619.15	0.877	−542.99
Preoperation	2	619.15		−619.15	0.769	−476.13
	1	29.08	486.93	457.85	0.675	309.05
	2	32.25	486.93	454.68	0.592	269.17
	3	38.61	486.93	448.32	0.519	232.68
	4	44.96	486.93	441.97	0.456	201.54
	5	44.96	486.93	441.97	0.400	176.79
	6	44.96	535.62	490.66	0.351	172.22
	7	44.96	535.62	490.66	0.308	151.12
	8	44.96	535.62	490.66	0.270	132.48
	9	44.96	535.62	490.66	0.237	116.29
	]0	44.96	535.62	490.66	0.208	102.06
	11	44.96	589.18	544.22	0.182	99.05
	12	44.96	589.18	544.22	0.160	87.08
	13	44.96	589.18	544.22	0.140	76.19
	14	44.96	589.18	544.22	0.123	66.94
	15	44.96	589.18	544.22	0.108	58.78
	16	44.96	648.10	603.14	0.095	57.30
	17	44.96	648.10	603.14	0.083	50.06
	18	44.96	648.10	603.14	0.073	44.03
	19	44.96	648.10	603.14	0.064	38.60
	20	44.96	648.10	603.14	0.056	33.78
	21	44.96	712.91	667.95	0.049	32.73
	22	44.96	712.91	667.95	0.043	28.72
	23	44.96	712.91	667.95	0.038	25.38
	24	44.96	712.91	667.95	0.033	22.04
	25	44.96	712.91	667.95	0.029	19.37
						906.33

Table 8.15 Calculation of present worth of net social benefit
(60% benefit and 14% discount rate)

End of year		Cash out	Cash in	NCF	$(pwf)^{14\%}$	$(DCF)^{14\%}$
Preoperation	0	678		−678	1	−678
Preoperation	1	619.15		−619.15	0.877	−542.99
Preoperation	2	619.15		−619.15	0.769	−476.13
	1	29.08	365.20	336.12	0.675	226.88
	2	32.25	365.20	332.95	0.592	197.11
	3	38.61	365.20	326.59	0.519	169.50
	4	44.96	365.20	320.24	0.456	146.03
	5	44.96	365.20	320.24	0.400	128.10
	6	44.96	401.72	356.76	0.351	125.22
	7	44.96	401.72	356.76	0.308	109.88
	8	44.96	401.72	356.76	0.270	96.33
	9	44.96	401.72	356.76	0.237	84.55
	10	44.96	401.72	356.76	0.208	74.21
	11	44.96	441.89	396.93	0.182	72.24
	12	44.96	441.89	396.93	0.160	63.51
	13	44.96	441.89	396.93	0.140	55.57
	14	44.96	441.89	396.93	0.123	48.82
	15	44.96	441.89	396.93	0.108	42.87
	16	44.96	486.08	441.12	0.095	41.91
	17	44.96	486.08	441.12	0.083	36.61
	18	44.96	486.08	441.12	0.073	32.20
	19	44.96	486.08	441.12	0.064	28.23
	20	44.96	486.08	441.12	0.056	24.70
	21	44.96	534.68	489.72	0.049	24.00
	22	44.96	534.68	489.72	0.043	21.06
	23	44.96	534.68	489.72	0.038	18.61
	24	44.96	534.68	489.72	0.033	16.16
	25	44.96	534.68	489.72	0.029	14.20
						201.18

Table 8.16 Calculation of present worth of net social benefit
(full benefit and 6% discount rate)

End of year		Cash out	Cash in	NCF	$(pwf)^{6\%}$	$(DCF)^{6\%}$
Preoperation	0	678		−678	1	−678
Preoperation	1	619.15		−619.15	0.943	−583.86
Preoperation	2	619.15		−619.15	0.890	−551.04
	1	29.08	608.66	579.58	0.840	486.85
	2	32.25	608.66	576.41	0.792	456.52
	3	38.61	608.66	570.05	0.747	425.83
	4	44.96	608.66	563.70	0.705	397.41
	5	44.96	608.66	563.70	0.665	374.86
	6	44.96	669.53	624.57	0.627	391.61
	7	44.96	669.53	624.57	0.592	369.75
	8	44.96	669.53	624.57	0.558	348.51
	9	44.96	669.53	624.57	0.527	329.15
	10	44.96	669.53	624.57	0.497	310.41
	11	44.96	736.48	691.52	0.469	324.32
	12	44.96	736.48	691.52	0.442	305.65
	13	44.96	736.48	691.52	0.417	288.36
	14	44.96	736.48	691.52	0.394	272.46
	15	44.96	736.48	691.52	0.371	256.55
	16	44.96	810.13	765.17	0.350	267.81
	17	44.96	810.13	765.17	0.331	253.27
	18	44.96	810.13	765.17	0.312	238.73
	19	44.96	810.13	765.17	0.294	224.96
	20	44.96	810.13	765.17	0.278	212.72
	21	44.96	891.14	846.18	0.262	221.70
	22	44.96	891.14	846.18	0.247	209.01
	23	44.96	891.14	846.18	0.233	197.16
	24	44.96	891.14	846.18	0.220	186.16
	25	44.96	891.14	846.18	0.207	175.16
						5,712.02

Table 8.17 Calculation of present worth of net social benefit (80%, benefit and 6% discount rate)

End of year		Cash out	Cash in	NCF	$(pwf)^{6\%}$	$(DCF)^{6\%}$
Preoperation	0	678		−678	1	−678
Preoperation	1	619.15		−619.15	0.943	−583.86
Preoperation	2	619.15		619.15	0.890	−551.04
	1	29.08	486.93	457.85	0.840	384.59
	2	32.25	486.93	454.68	0.792	360.11
	3	38.61	486.93	448.32	0.747	334.90
	4	44.96	486.93	441.97	0.705	311.59
	5	44.96	486.93	441.97	0.665	293.91
	6	44.96	535.62	490.66	0.627	307.64
	7	44.96	535.62	490.66	0.592	290.47
	8	44.96	535.62	490.66	0.558	273.79
	9	44.96	535.62	490.66	0.527	258.58
	10	44.96	535.62	490.66	0.497	243.86
	11	44.96	589.18	544.22	0.469	255.24
	12	44.96	589.18	544.22	0.442	240.55
	13	44.96	589.18	544.22	0.417	226.94
	14	44.96	589.18	544.22	0.394	214.42
	15	44.96	589.18	544.22	0.371	210.91
	16	44.96	648.10	603.14	0.350	211.10
	17	44.96	648.10	603.14	0.331	199.64
	18	44.96	648.10	603.14	0.312	188.18
	19	44.96	648.10	603.14	0.294	177.32
	20	44.96	648.10	603.14	0.278	167.67
	21	44.96	712.91	667.95	0.262	175.00
	22	44.96	712.91	667.95	0.247	164.98
	23	44.96	712.91	667.95	0.233	155.63
	24	44.96	712.91	667.95	0.220	146.95
	25	44.96	712.91	667.95	0.207	<u>138.27</u>
						4,110.34

Table 8.18 Calculation of present worth of net social benefit
(60% benefit and 6% discount rate)

End of year		Cash out	Cash in	NCF	$(pwf)^{6\%}$	$(DCF)^{6\%}$
Preoperation	0	678		−678	1	−678
Preoperation	1	619.15		−619.15	0.943	−583.86
Preoperation	2	619.15		−619.15	0.890	−551.04
	1	29.08	365.20	336.12	0.840	282.34
	2	32.25	365.20	332.95	0.792	263.70
	3	38.61	365.20	326.59	0.747	243.96
	4	44.96	365.20	320.24	0.705	225.77
	5	44.96	365.20	320.24	0.665	212.96
	6	44.96	401.72	356.76	0.627	223.69
	7	44.96	401.72	356.76	0.592	211.20
	8	44.96	401.72	356.76	0.558	199.07
	9	44.96	401.72	356.76	0.527	188.01
	10	44.96	401.72	356.76	0.497	177.31
	11	44.96	441.89	396.93	0.469	186.16
	12	44.96	441.89	396.93	0.442	175.44
	13	44.96	441.89	396.93	0.417	165.52
	14	44.96	441.89	396.93	0.394	156.39
	15	44.96	441.89	396.93	0.371	147.26
	16	44.96	486.08	441.12	0.350	154.39
	17	44.96	486.08	441.12	0.331	146.01
	18	44.96	486.08	441.12	0.312	137.63
	19	44.96	486.08	441.12	0.294	129.69
	20	44.96	486.08	441.12	0.278	122.63
	21	44.96	534.68	489.72	0.262	128.31
	22	44.96	534.68	489.72	0.247	120.96
	23	44.96	534.68	489.72	0.233	114.10
	24	44.96	534.68	489.72	0.220	107.74
	25	44.96	534.68	489.72	0.207	101.37
						2,508.71

8.7 Exercise

This exercise is a case study originally used as training material in the project feasibility study training course organized by the Asian Productivity Organization, who kindly approved the inclusion of it in this book. The problem is reproduced here and the reader is strongly advised to attempt to do it. They will be able to fully understand the concepts underlaid in financial and economic analysis after going through this exercise.

8.7.1 Background

The Caribe Development Finance Company (CDFC) and the Ministry of Industry (MOI) have been simultaneously approached by the promoters of a glass containers project. The promoters propose to build a jar manufacturing plant to supply containers to the domestic market of the Island of Caribe. The name of the proposed company is Caribe Containers Corporation. The Corporation hopes to take over the container market now being supplied by imported jars from the United States. Current and future local use of jars is expected to remain at a level amounting to a CIF value of US$950,000.00 per year for the next decade. Of the total jar imports, approximately 85% are used by a local pickle processing firm, Caribe Pickles Company. The remaining 15% is sold in the local market for home and commercial uses.

The promoters of Caribe Containers Corporation have asked Caribe Development Finance Company (CDFC) for a loan to assist in financing project costs at an interest rate of 12%. At the same time, they have applied to MOI for tariff protection under provisions of the Infant Industries Protection Act recently enacted. To make a reasonable return on investment, the promoters argue that at least 35% tariff should be imposed on the CIF value of imported jars. Their financial statements have been drawn up under the assumption that a 35% protective tariff would be imposed and that the project would then be locally competitive. The tariff would increase the local price of imported containers by 35%.

8.7.2 Problem

The MOI and CDFC have set up a small joint committee to study the container proposal. Assuming that you are a member of that committee, you are asked to do the following:

Financial analysis

(a) Calculate the financial-IRR (FIRR) on all resources (all equity case) invested in the project, assuming a 35% tariff on imported jars.
(b) Calculate the financial-IRR (FIRR) on all resources (all equity case) invested in the project, assuming no tariff on imported jars.

Economic analysis

(c) Calculate the economic-IRR (EIRR) of the project.
(d) Be prepared to discuss means for reshaping the proposal to minimize the adverse effects on other parties. Do you recommend that the proposal be approved? In its present form? In a reshaped form?

In addition to the information described under "Background", more data are given in Tables 8.20–8.24. Additional data are provided in the following section.

8.7.3 Basic information

a. Land

The container manufacturing plant will be built on 10 hectares of agricultural land very near the Caribe Pickles packing plant. The land is currently used for growing cucumbers and yields a net income of C$1,500.00 per hectare per year. The land is beyond the urban fringe, and without the project it would continue to be used for agricultural production for at least 10 more years. The land (10 hectares) has already been purchased by the Corporation at a price of C$13,000.00 per hectare.

b. Transport to market

The primary markets for the Corporation's output will be Caribe Pickles Company which is located nearby and can be served with negligible transport costs, and wholesalers in the capital city 30 miles away who will pick up the containers at the plant.

c. Exchange rate

The official exchange rate (OER) is US$1.00 = C$3.00. The shadow exchange rate (SER) is US$1.00 = C$3.45.

d. Years of operation and terminal values

Construction would be in 2002. Operations would take place during 2003–2012. At the end of the 2012 operational year, the machinery and equipment would reach the end of its rated life. The Containers Corporation could either reinvest in 2013, or it could salvage the land, buildings, machinery and equipment, and working capital. Re-investment would require a new appraisal to be made in 2012. For our purposes, work on the assumption that the assets will be salvaged at the end of 2012.

(1) *Machinery and equipment*: Salvage value in 2012 is estimated at C$25,000.00 However, C$10,000.00 would be required to dismantle and get the equipment to saleability (Table 8.20).
(2) *Buildings*: In 2012 the buildings could be converted into a flat storage area. A warehouse of equivalent size currently costs C$200,000.00 to construct. Conversion of the buildings to a warehouse would cost C$20,000.00 (Table 8.20).
(3) *Land*: The land could be resold along with the warehouse at the expected market price of C$13,000.00 per hectare (Table 8.20).
(4) *Working capital*: The working capital can be treated as a salvaged item in 2012 and added to project benefits. In fact, working capital will not be salvaged as such in 2012. Rather, it will be used up by the project and will not be replaced, since there will be no production in 2013. The project's production cost will be lower in 2012 because (rather than ordering more direct materials) the project will use up its inventories in producing its final two months of output. The recovery of working capital can be treated as either a reduction in production cost in 2012 or as a salvage value in 2012. Either way, the *net* cash flow will be the same.

e. Production costs

Production will begin in 2003. We are assuming that build-up to full production will be immediate. This is obviously a simplification. The production costs will be the same from 2003 through 2012 (Table 8.21).

f. Pre operating expenses

These consist of administration and overhead expenses during the construction period and minimal trial operating expenses. Interest during construction is payable only after operations begin.

g. Working capital

Working capital requirements are calculated as a fraction of annual production costs. In this case, two months' requirements for production are included in working capital.

h. Silica, aggregates and sand

This is the largest single item of working capital as well as production costs. Because of its size and importance in the project, the project's initial analysts conferred with the Caribe Mining Company to determine whether the required materials could be provided and at what cost. The Mining Company reported that they would have to buy additional (imported) equipment and hire more machinery operators to meet the Containers Corporation's needs. Because the silica, aggregates and sand represent a large item of cost, and because their purchase causes substantial indirect use of foreign exchange, the MOI staff members who previewed the original application asked for a breakdown of the Mining Company's costs. The breakdown of the Mining company's costs is given in the following table:

Table 8.19 Breakdown of mining company's costs (C$ $\times$ 10^3)

Item	Foreign exchnage (at OER)	Local currency	Total
Imported mining machinery and trucks			
a. CIF cost	473.0	–	473.0
b. Tariff	–	142.6	142.6
c. Local transport	–	32.4	32.4
Skilled machinery operators	–	388.8	388.8
Fuel* (for trucks and machinery)	–	68.0	68.0
Maintenance(for trucks and machinery)	24.0	20.0	44.0
Overheads and profits	–	150.4	150.4
Total	497.0	802.2	1,299.2

*Fuel is exported by the country.

i. Labour

Skilled labour is in tight supply throughout the country. Unskilled labour in the project area would be available from among hired farm labourers, who currently are paid cash wages and wages in kind (lunch and cigarettes) which altogether amounts (on average) to the equivalent of one half of the wages they will be paid by Caribe Containers Corporation and by the construction company (Tables 8.20 and 8.21). Labourers working in the construction and manufacturing industries are covered by a minimum wage law. The minimum wage is currently approximately double the wage paid in non-covered jobs.

j. Utilities

(1) *Electricity*: This is valued at roughly its opportunity costs, according to a recent study done jointly by the Planning Office and the Utilities Regulating Commission (Table 8.21).
(2) *Water*: The pricing study is currently underway. A World Bank mission has recently argued that water is underpriced relative to its replacement cost. The results of the study will not be available for several months. Since water is a small part of production cost, and since we do not know the actual cost, you can simply take the price paid as the economic cost (Table 8.21).
(3) *Fuel*: The type used by the project is currently being exported at FOB prices 30% above the price paid by domestic users such as Caribe Containers Corporation. The country is a small net exporter of petroleum products compared to other producers. Petroleum exports amount to roughly 10% of the country's total exports in value terms. The fuel supplier is a parastatal corporation whose operating deficits are covered by the government. Current policy is to fill all domestic demands for fuel at the subsidised price of C$68.00 per barrel and export the remainder of sustained yield production at the prevailing export price of C$88.40.

k. Market

Caribe Containers Corporation hopes to take over most if not all of the domestic market for glass containers. The silica available domestically is of good quality and the quantity is sufficient to meet the project needs. The quality of the containers is expected to be competitive with the imported containers. With a slight price advantage (due to the proposed import tariff) and with the shorter delivery time enjoyed by the local production, the Corporation hopes to capture the local market quickly. The proposed 35% tariff would raise the landed cost of imported containers to C$3,949,500.00

per year (i.e. C$12.47 per dozen). The container company plans to gain a price advantage over imported containers by selling at a price of C$3,850,000.00 (i.e. C$12.15 per dozen). The domestic market has increased only slightly in recent years, and the corporation expects the market to remain fairly static. If the market grows, then the plan is to let imports fill the extra demand in the short run. If the market grows sufficiently, and if the present plant is profitable, the Caribe Containers Corporation would later consider an expansion project. The present project is based on the conservative assumption of no growth in the domestic market (Table 8.24).

I. Sale of pickles

Caribe Pickles, the company which purchases 85% of the imported containers, is currently exporting 98% of its pickle output to the United States, where it enjoys a slight cost advantage in the Southeastern U.S. market. Caribe Pickles is 90% foreign-owned (a major U.S. food processing firm).

The pickles company is in its 5th year of successful operations in the country. The Island of Caribe was selected as the site for the U.S. company's pickle packaging operations because of increasing labour costs in the U.S. Several other countries in addition to Caribe were investigated as potential locations before the U.S. company selected Caribe as the site for its overseas packaging plant. At the time of the decision to locate the packaging plant in Caribe, the government of Caribe assured the American company that there would be no new taxes or policy changes which would be detrimental to the operations of the packaging plant.

Table 8.20 Breakdown of project costs (2002) (C$ × 10³)

	Foreign exchange (at OER)	Local currency	Total
1. Land		130.0	130.0
2. Buildings			
a. Steel			
(i) CIF	81.4	–	81.4
(ii) Tariff	–	32.6	32.6
b. Cement			
(i) CIF	35.8	–	35.8
(ii) Tariff		7.2	7.2
c. Local transport (steel & cement)	–	6.0	6.0
d Local materials	–	22.0	22.0
e Skilled labour	–	18.0	18.0
f. Unskilled labour	–	74.0	74.0
g. Overhead and miscellaneous	–	93.0	93.0
3. Machinery and equipment (for jar mfg.)			
a. CIF (includes installation by supplier)	401.9	–	401.9
b. Tariff	–	120.6	120.6
c. Local transport (port to factory)	–	27.5	27.5
4. Working capital*	74.1	474.4	548.5
5. Preoperating expenses	–	25.0	25.0
Total	593.2	1,030.3	1,623.5

*Two months of production costs

Table 8.21 Breakdown of annual production costs
for each year 2003–2012 (C$ × 10³)

	Foreign exchange (at OER)	Local currency	Total
1. Direct materials			
a. Silica, aggregates and sand*	–	1299.2	1299.2
b. Metal Covers			
(i) CIF	444.8	–	444.8
(ii) Tariff	–	89.0	89.0
(iii) Local transport (port to factory)	–	22.2	22.2
2. Utilities			
a. Electricity	–	11.0	11.0
b. Water	–	11.0	11.0
c. Fuel (500 barrels)	–	34.0	34.0
3. Labour			
a. Technical and skilled	–	464.0	464.0
b. Unskilled	–	696.0	696.0
4. Taxes	–	220.0	220.0
Total**	444.8	2,846.4	3,291.2

* See Table 8.19 before shadow pricing this.
** Note that interest and depreciation are not included, since we are working on the basis of all equity capital.

Table 8.22 Annual sales revenue 2003–2012,
assuming 35% tariff protection (C$ × 10³)

	Foreign exchange (at OER)	Local currency	Total
Annual sales revenue (317,000 dozen at C$12.15/dozen)	–	3,850.0	3,850.0

Table 8.23 Alternative cost of imported containers (C$ × 10³)

	Foreign exchange (at OER)	Local currency	Total
CIF (US$950.0 × C$3.0)	2,850.0	–	2,850.0
Tariff (35% on CIF)	–	997.5	997.5
Local handling and transport from port to markets	–	102.0	102.0
Total	2850.0	1,099.5	3,949.5

Table 8.24 Market analysis and price data

	2002 (million units)	2003–2011 (million units)	2012 (million units)
Domestic use	3.8	3.8	3.8
Caribe Pickles	3.23	3.23	3.23
Other	0.57	0.57	0.57
Domestic Production	0	3.8	3.8
Caribe Containers	0	3.8	3.8
Other	0	0	0
Imports	3.8	0	0

Price Data

Imported Jars
(Quart size, wide mouth with lids)

CIF	US $0.25/unit	or	US $3.00/dozen
(at OER)	C $0.75/unit	or	C $9.00/dozen
Tariff	C $0.2625/unit	or	C $3.15/dozen
Local handling and transport	C $0.0268/unit	or	C $0.322/dozen
Delivered price	C $1.039/unit	or	C $12.47/dozen
Proposed price for project output	C $1.01/unit	or	C $12.15/dozen

Solution

The solution to parts (a), (b) and (c) are given below. Part (d) is left for the readers to solve.

Financial analysis

(a)   Calculate the financial-IRR (FIRR) on all resources (all equity case) invested in the project, assuming a 35% tariff on imported jars.

Cost
(i)   Annual production cost   = 3,291.2
(ii) Project cost   = 1,623.5 (including working capital)

   Note: Working capital   = 1/6 of production cost
                                        = 3,291.2/6 = 548.5

Benefits
Sales   = 3,850 (i.e. at 12.15/dozen)
Salvage = 873.5 (at the end of year 10)

   873.5 is obtained as follows:
Mechinery and equipment	25
less dismantliing cost	−10
Building converted to warehouse	200
less conversion cost	−20
Land	130
Working capital	548.5
Total	873.5

End of year	Cost			Benefit			Net cash flow (NCF)
	Capital	Production	Total	Sales	Salvage	Total	
0	1,623.5						(1,623.5)
1		3,291.2		3,850			558.8
2		3,291.2		3,850			558.8
3		3,291.2		3,850			558.8
4		3,291.2		3,850			558.8
5		3,291.2		3,850			558.8
6		3,291.2		3,850			558.8
7		3,291.2		3,850			558.8
8		3.291.2		3,850			558.8
9		3,291.2		3,850			558.8
10		3,291.2		3,850	873.5		1,432.3

FIRR = 33% (approx.)

(b) Calculate the financial-IRR (FIRR) on all resources (all equity case) invested in the project, assuming no tariff on imported jars.

Cost
(i)   Annual production cost $= 3,291.2 - 220 \text{ (tax)} = 3,071.2$
(ii) Project cost $= 1,623.5$

Benefits

Sales $= 3,850 \times \dfrac{12.15 - 3.15 \text{ (tariff)}}{12.15} = 3,850 \times \dfrac{9}{12.15}$

          $= 2,852$ (i.e. at 9/dozen)   in order to be competitive

Salvage $= 873.5$ (at the end of year 10)

End of year	Cost			Benefit			Net cash flow (NCF)
	Capital	Production	Total	Sales	Salvage	Total	
0	1,623.5						(1,623.5)
1		3,071.2		2,852			(219.2)
2		3,071.2		2,852			(219.2)
3		3,071.2		2,852			(219.2)
4		3,071.2		2,852			(219.2)
5		3,071.2		2,852			(219.2)
6		3,071.2		2,852			(219.2)
7		3,071.2		2,852			(219.2)
8		3,071.2		2,852			(219.2)
9		3,071.2		2,852			(219.2)
10		3,071.2		2,852	873.5		654.3

FIRR = negative value

Economic analysis

(c) Calculate the economic-IRR (EIRR) of the project.

Cost
(i)   Mining company's cost = 1,251.6 (shadowed)

    1251.6 is obtained as follows:

Imported machinery, etc. CIF	=	544	(3.45/3.00) × 473
Tariff		0	(ignored)
Local transport		32.4	
Skill operators		388.8	
Fuel		88.4	(opportunity cost)
Maintence		47.6	(3.45/3.00) × 24 + 20
Overhead		150.4	
	Total	1,251.6	

(ii) Annual production cost = 2,663.5 (shadowed)

    2,663.5 is obtained as follows:

1. Direct materials
   a. Silica, aggregates and sand   1,251.6
   b. Metal covers
      (i)   CIF   511.5
      (ii) Tariff   0
      (iii) Local transport   22.2
            (port to factory)
2. Utilities
   a. Electricity   11.0
   b. Water   11.0
   c. Fuel   44.2
3. Labour
   a. Technical and skilled   464
   b. Unskilled (50% shadow cost)   348
4. Taxes   0

                      Total   2,663.5

(iii) Project cost = 1,269.4 (shadowed)

1,269.4 is obtained as follows:

1. Land		0	
2. Building			
a. Steel			
(i) CIF		93.6	
(ii) Tariff		0	
b. Cement			
(i) CIF		41.2	
(ii) Tariff		0	
c. Local transport (steel and cement)		6	
d. Local materials		22	
e. Skilled labour		18	
f. Unskilled labour (50% shadow cost)		37	
g. Overhead and miscellaneous		93	
3. Machinery and equipment (for jar mfg.)			
a. CIF (includes installation by supplier)		462.2	(3.45/3.00) × 401.9
b. Tariff		0	
c. Local transport (port to factory)		27.5	
4. Working capital		443.9	(1/6 of production cost of 2,663.5)
5. Preoperating expenses		25	
	Total	1,269.4	

Benefits

(iv) Opportunity cost = 3,379.5 (shadowed)

3,379.5 is obtained as follows:

CIF = 2,850 × 3.45/3.00 (currency) =	3,277.5	
Tariff	0	
Local handling and transport From port to markets	102	
Total	3,379.5	

(v)   Savage value = 638.9 (shadowed)

  638.9 is obtained as follows:
Machinery and equipment	25
Less dismantling cost	−10
Building converted to warehouse	200
Less conversion cost	0
Working capital	
= 1/6 of production cost	
= 2,663.5/6 =	443.9
Total	638.9

End of year	Cost Capital	Production	Crop (or land)	Total	Benefit Opportunity cost	Salvage	Total	Net cash flow (NCF)
0	1,269.4							(1,269.4)
1		2,663.5	15		3,379.5			701
2		2,663.5	15		3,379.5			701
3		2,663.5	15		3,379.5			701
4		2,663.5	15		3,379.5			701
5		2,663.5	15		3,379.5			701
6		2,663.5	15		3,379.5			701
7		2,663.5	15		3,379.5			701
8		2,663.5	15		3,379.5			701
9		2,663.5	15		3,379.5			701
10		2,663.5	15		3,379.5	638.9		1339.9

EIRR = 55% (approx.)

Readers should note that there is only one EIRR for this project. Different financial arrangements (e.g. changing the percentage of tariff) will only change the FIRR but not the EIRR.

Appendix 1
Compound Interest Tables

$$i = 1\%$$

n	caf $(1 + i)^n$	pwf $\dfrac{1}{(1+i)^n}$	uscaf $\dfrac{(1+i)^n - 1}{i}$	ussff $\dfrac{1}{(1+i)^n - 1}$	uspwf $\dfrac{(1+i)^n - 1}{i(1+i)^n}$	uscrf $\dfrac{i(1+i)^n}{(1+i)^n - 1}$
1	1.0100	0.9901	1.0000	1.0000	0.9901	1.0100
2	1.0201	0.9803	2.0100	0.4975	1.9704	0.5075
3	1.0303	0.9706	3.0301	0.3300	2.9410	0.3400
4	1.0406	0.9610	4.0604	0.2463	3.9020	0.2563
5	1.0510	0.9515	5.1010	0.1960	4.8534	0.2060
6	1.0615	0.9420	6.1520	0.1625	5.7955	0.1725
7	1.0721	0.9327	7.2135	0.1386	6.7282	0.1486
8	1.0829	0.9235	8.2857	0.1207	7.6517	0.1307
9	1.0937	0.9143	9.3685	0.1067	8.5660	0.1167
10	1.1046	0.9053	10.462	0.0956	9.4713	0.1056
11	1.1157	0.8963	11.567	0.0865	10.368	0.0965
12	1.1268	0.8874	12.683	0.0788	11.255	0.0888
13	1.1381	0.8787	13.809	0.0724	12.134	0.0824
14	1.1495	0.8700	14.947	0.0669	13.004	0.0769
15	1.1610	0.8613	16.097	0.0621	13.865	0.0721
16	1.1726	0.8528	17.258	0.0579	14.718	0.0679
17	1.1843	0.8444	18.430	0.0543	15.562	0.0643
18	1.1961	0.8360	19.615	0.0510	16.398	0.0610
19	1.2081	0.8277	20.8.11	0.0481	17.226	0.0581
20	1.2202	0.8195	22.019	0.0454	18.046	0.0554
21	1.2324	0.8114	23.239	0.0430	18.857	0.0530
22	1.2447	0.8034	24.472	0.0409	19.660	0.0509
23	1.2572	0.7954	25.716	0.0389	20.456	0.0489
24	1.2697	0.7876	26.973	0.0371	21.243	0.0471
25	1.2824	0.7798	28.243	0.0354	22.023	0.0454
26	1.2953	0.7720	29.526	0.0339	22.795	0.0439
27	1.3082	0.7644	30.821	0.0324	23.560	0.0424
28	1.3213	0.7568	32.129	0.0311	24.316	0.0411
29	1.3345	0.7493	33.450	0.0299	25.066	0.0399
30	1.3478	1.7419	34.785	0.0287	25.808	0.0387

$$i = 2\%$$

n	caf $(1+i)^n$	pwf $\dfrac{1}{(1+i)^n}$	uscaf $\dfrac{(1+i)^n-1}{i}$	ussff $\dfrac{1}{(1+i)^n-1}$	uspwf $\dfrac{(1+i)^n-1}{i(1+i)^n}$	uscrf $\dfrac{i(1+i)^n}{(1+i)^n-1}$
1	1.0200	0.9804	1.0000	1.0000	0.9804	1.0200
2	1.0404	0.9612	2.0200	0.4950	1.9416	0.5150
3	1.0612	0.9423	3.0604	0.3268	2.8839	0.3468
4	1.0824	0.9238	4.1216	0.2426	3.8077	0.2626
5	1.1041	0.9057	5.2040	0.1922	4.7135	0.2122
6	1.1262	0.8880	6.3081	0.1585	5.6014	0.1785
7	1.1487	0.8706	7.4343	0.1345	6.4720	0.1545
8	1.1717	0.8535	8.5830	0.1165	7.3255	0.1365
9	1.1951	0.8368	9.7546	0.1025	8.1622	0.1225
10	1.2190	0.8203	10.950	0.0913	8.9826	0.1113
11	1.2434	0.8043	12.169	0.0822	9.7868	0.1022
12	1.2682	0.7885	13.412	0.0746	10.575	0.0946
13	1.2936	0.7730	14.680	0.0681	11.348	0.0881
14	1.3195	0.7579	15.947	0.0626	12.106	0.0826
15	1.3459	0.7430	17.293	0.0578	12.849	0.0778
16	1.3728	0.7284	18.639	0.0537	13.578	0.0737
17	1.4002	0.7142	20.012	0.0500	14.292	0.0700
18	1.4282	0.7002	21.412	0.0467	14.992	0.0667
19	1.4568	0.6864	22.841	0.0438	15.678	0.0638
20	1.4859	0.6730	24.297	0.0412	16.351	0.0612
21	1.5157	0.6598	25.783	0.0388	17.011	0.0588
22	1.5460	0.6468	27.299	0.0366	17.658	0.0566
23	1.5769	0.6342	28.845	0.0347	18.292	0.0547
24	1.6084	0.6217	30.422	0.0329	18.914	0.0529
25	1.6406	0.6095	32.030	0.0312	19.523	0.0512
26	1.6734	0.5976	33.671	0.0297	20.121	0.0497
27	1.7069	0.5859	35.344	0.0283	20.707	0.0483
28	1.7410	0.5744	37.051	0.0270	21.281	0.0470
29	1.7758	0.5631	38.792	0.0258	21.844	0.0458
30	1.8114	1.5521	40.568	0.0246	22.396	0.0446

$$i = 3\%$$

n	caf $(1 + i)^n$	pwf $\dfrac{1}{(1+i)^n}$	uscaf $\dfrac{(1+i)^n -1}{i}$	ussff $\dfrac{1}{(1+i)^n -1}$	uspwf $\dfrac{(1+i)^n -1}{i(1+i)^n}$	uscrf $\dfrac{i(1+i)^n}{(1+i)^n -1}$
1	1.0300	0.9709	1.0000	1.0000	0.9709	1.0300
2	1.0609	0.9426	2.0300	0.4926	1.9135	0.5226
3	1.0927	0.9151	3.0909	0.3235	2.8286	0.3535
4	1.1255	0.8885	4.1836	0.2390	3.7171	0.2690
5	1.1593	0.8626	5.3091	0.1884	4.5797	0.2184
6	1.1941	0.8375	6.4648	0.1546	5.4172	0.1846
7	1.2299	0.8131	7.6625	0.1305	6.2303	0.1605
8	1.2668	0.7894	8.8923	0.1125	7.0197	0.1425
9	1.3048	0.7664	10.159	0.0984	7.7861	0.1284
10	1.3439	0.7441	11.464	0.0872	8.5302	0.1172
11	1.3842	0.7224	12.808	0.0781	9.2526	0.1081
12	1.4258	0.7014	14.192	0.0705	9.9540	0.1005
13	1.4685	0.6810	15.618	0.0640	10.635	0.0940
14	1.5126	0.6611	17.086	0.0585	11.296	0.0885
15	1.5580	0.6419	18.599	0.0538	11.938	0.0838
16	1.6047	0.6232	20.157	0.0496	12.561	0.0796
17	1.6528	0.6050	21.762	0.0460	13.166	0.0760
18	1.7024	0.5874	23.414	0.0427	13.754	0.0727
19	1.7535	0.5703	25.117	0.0398	14.324	0.0698
20	1.8061	0.5537	26.870	0.0372	14.877	0.0672
21	1.8603	0.5375	28.676	0.0349	15.415	0.0649
22	1.9161	0.5219	30.537	0.0327	15.937	0.0627
23	1.9736	0.5067	32.453	0.0308	16.444	0.0608
24	2.0328	0.4919	34.426	0.0290	16.936	0.0590
25	2.0938	0.4776	36.459	0.0274	17.413	0.0574
26	2.1566	0.4637	38.553	0.0259	17.877	0.0559
27	2.2213	0.4502	40.710	0.0246	18.327	0.0546
28	2.2879	0.4371	42.931	0.0233	18.764	0.0533
29	2.3566	0.4243	45.219	0.0221	19.188	0.0521
30	2.4273	0.4120	47.575	0.0210	19.600	0.0510

$$i = 4\%$$

n	caf $(1+i)^n$	pwf $\dfrac{1}{(1+i)^n}$	uscaf $\dfrac{(1+i)^n-1}{i}$	ussff $\dfrac{1}{(1+i)^n-1}$	uspwf $\dfrac{(1+i)^n-1}{i(1+i)^n}$	uscrf $\dfrac{i(1+i)^n}{(1+i)^n-1}$
1	1.0400	0.9615	1.0000	1.0000	0.9615	1.0400
2	1.0816	0.9246	2.0400	0.4902	1.8661	0.5302
3	1.1249	0.8890	3.1216	0.3203	2.7751	0.3603
4	1.1699	0.8548	4.2465	0.2355	3.6299	0.2755
5	1.2167	0.8219	5.4163	0.1846	4.4518	0.2246
6	1.2653	0.7903	6.6330	0.1508	5.2421	0.1908
7	1.3159	0.7599	7.8983	0.1266	6.0021	0.1666
8	1.3686	0.7307	9.2142	0.1085	6.7327	0.1485
9	1.4233	0.7026	10.583	0.0945	7.4353	0.1345
10	1.4802	0.6756	12.006	0.0833	8.1109	0.1233
11	1.5395	0.6496	13.486	0.0741	8.7605	0.1141
12	1.6010	0.6246	15.026	0.0666	9.3851	0.1066
13	1.6651	0.6006	16.627	0.0601	9.9856	0.1001
14	1.7317	0.5775	18.292	0.0547	10.563	0.0947
15	1.8009	0.5553	20.024	0.0499	11.118	0.0899
16	1.8730	0.5339	21.825	0.0458	11.652	0.0858
17	1.9479	0.5134	23.698	0.0422	12.166	0.0822
18	2.0258	0.4936	25.645	0.0390	12.659	0.0790
19	2.1068	0.4746	27.671	0.0361	13.134	0.0761
20	2.1911	0.4564	29.778	0.0336	13.590	0.0736
21	2.2788	0.4388	31.969	0.0313	14.029	0.0713
22	2.3699	0.4220	34.248	0.0292	14.451	0.0692
23	2.4647	0.4057	36.618	0.0273	14.857	0.0673
24	2.5633	0.3901	39.083	0.0256	15.247	0.0656
25	2.6658	0.3751	41.646	0.0240	15.622	0.0640
26	2.7725	0.3607	44.312	0.0226	15.983	0.0626
27	2.8834	0.3468	47.084	0.0212	16.330	0.0612
28	2..9987	0.3335	49.968	0.0200	16.663	0.0600
29	3.1187	0.3207	52.966	0.0189	16.984	0.0589
30	3.2434	0.3083	56.085	0.0178	17.292	0.0578

$$i = 5\%$$

n	caf $(1 + i)^n$	pwf $\dfrac{1}{(1+i)^n}$	uscaf $\dfrac{(1+i)^n - 1}{i}$	ussff $\dfrac{1}{(1+i)^n - 1}$	uspwf $\dfrac{(1+i)^n - 1}{i(1+i)^n}$	uscrf $\dfrac{i(1+i)^n}{(1+i)^n - 1}$
1	1.0500	0.9524	1.0000	1.0000	0.9524	1.0500
2	1.1025	0.9070	2.0500	0.4878	1.8594	0.5378
3	1.1576	0.8638	3.1525	0.3172	2.7232	0.3672
4	1.2155	0.8227	4.3101	0.2320	3.5460	0.2820
5	1.2763	0.7835	5.5256	0.1810	4.3295	0.2310
6	1.3401	0.7462	6.8019	0.1470	5.0757	0.1970
7	1.4071	0.7107	8.1420	0.1228	5.7864	0.1728
8	1.4775	0.6768	9.5491	0.1047	6.4632	0.1547
9	1.5513	0.6446	11.027	0.0907	7.1078	0.1407
10	1.6289	0.6139	12.578	0.0795	7.7217	0.1295
11	1.7103	0.5847	14.207	0.0704	8.3064	0.1204
12	1.7959	0.5568	15.917	0.0628	8.8633	0.1128
13	1.8856	0.5303	17.713	0.0565	9.3936	0.1065
14	1.9799	0.5051	19.599	0.0510	9.8986	0.1010
15	2.0789	0.4810	21.579	0.0463	10.380	0.0963
16	2.1829	0.4581	23.657	0.0423	10.838	0.0923
17	2.2920	0.4363	25.840	0.0387	11.274	0.0887
18	2.4066	0.4155	28.132	0.0355	11.690	0.0855
19	2.5270	0.3957	30.539	0.0327	12.085	0.0827
20	2.6533	0.3769	33.066	0.0302	12.462	0.0802
21	2.7860	0.3589	35.719	0.0280	12.821	0.0780
22	2.9253	0.3418	38.505	0.0260	13.163	0.0760
23	3.0715	0.3256	41.430	0.0241	13.489	0.0741
24	3.2251	0.3101	44.502	0.0225	13.799	0.0725
25	3.3864	0.2953	47.727	0.0210	14.094	0.0710
26	3.5557	0.2812	51.113	0.0196	13.375	0.0696
27	3.7335	0.2678	54.669	0.0183	14.643	0.0683
28	3.9201	0.2551	58.403	0.0171	14.898	0.0671
29	4.1161	0.2429	62.323	0.0160	15.141	0.0660
30	4.3219	0.2314	66.439	0.0151	15.372	0.0651

$$i = 6\%$$

n	caf $(1+i)^n$	pwf $\dfrac{1}{(1+i)^n}$	uscaf $\dfrac{(1+i)^n-1}{i}$	ussff $\dfrac{1}{(1+i)^n-1}$	uspwf $\dfrac{(1+i)^n-1}{i(1+i)^n}$	uscrf $\dfrac{i(1+i)^n}{(1+i)^n-1}$
1	1.0600	0.9434	1.0000	1.0000	0.9434	1.0600
2	1.1236	0.8900	2.0600	0.4854	1.8334	0.5454
3	1.1910	0.8396	3.1836	0.3141	2.6730	0.3741
4	1.2625	0.7921	4.3746	0.2286	3.4651	0.2886
5	1.3382	0.7473	5.6371	0.1774	4.2124	0.2374
6	1.4185	0.7050	6.9753	0.1434	4.9173	0.2034
7	1.5036	0.6651	8.3938	0.1191	5.5824	0.1791
8	1.5938	0.6274	9.8975	0.1010	6.2098	0.1610
9	1.6895	0.5919	11.491	0.0870	6.8017	0.1470
10	1.7908	0.5584	13.181	0.0759	7.3601	0.1359
11	1.8983	0.5268	14.972	0.0668	7.8869	0.1268
12	2.0122	0.4970	16.870	0.0593	8.3838	0.1193
13	2.1329	0.4688	18.882	0.0530	8.8527	0.1130
14	2.2609	0.4423	21.015	0.0476	9.2950	0.1076
15	2.3966	0:4173	23.276	0.0430	9.7122	0.1030
16	2.5404	0.3936	25.673	0.0390	10.106	0.0990
17	2.6928	0.3714	28.213	0.0354	10.477	0.0954
18	2.8543	0.3503	30.906	0.0324	10.828	0.0924
19	3.0256	0.3305	33.760	0.0296	11.158	0.0896
20	3.2071	0.3118	36.786	0.0272	11.470	0.0872
21	3.3996	0.2942	39.993	0.0250	11.764	0.0850
22	3.6035	0.2775	43.392	0.0230	12.042	0.0830
23	3.8197	0.2618	46.996	0.0213	12.303	0.0813
24	4.0489	0.2470	50.816	0.0197	12.550	0.0797
25	4.2919	0.2330	54.865	0.0182	12.783	0.0782
26	4.5494	0.2198	59.156	0.0169	13.003	0.0769
27	4.8223	0.2074	63.706	0.0157	13.211	0.0757
28	5.1117	0.1956	68.528	0.0146	13.406	0.0746
29	5.4184	0.1846	73.640	0.0136	13.591	0.0736
30	5.7435	0.1741	79.058	0.0126	13.765	0.0726

$$i = 7\%$$

n	caf $(1+i)^n$	pwf $\dfrac{1}{(1+i)^n}$	uscaf $\dfrac{(1+i)^n-1}{i}$	ussff $\dfrac{1}{(1+i)^n-1}$	uspwf $\dfrac{(1+i)^n-1}{i(1+i)^n}$	uscrf $\dfrac{i(1+i)^n}{(1+i)^n-1}$
1	1.0700	0.9346	1.0000	1.0000	0.9346	1.0700
2	1.1449	0.8734	2.0700	0.4831	1.8080	0.5531
3	1.2250	0.8163	3.2149	0.3111	2.6243	0.3811
4	1.3108	0.7629	4.4399	0.2252	3.3872	0.2952
5	1.4026	0.7130	5.7507	0.1739	4.1002	0.2439
6	1.5007	0.6663	7.1533	0.1398	4.7665	0.2098
7	1.6058	0.6227	8.6540	0.1156	5.3893	0.1856
8	1.7182	0.5820	10.260	0.0975	5.9713	0.1675
9	1.8385	0.5439	11.978	0.0835	6.5152	0.1535
10	1.9672	0.5083	13.816	0.0724	7.0236	0.1424
11	2.1049	0.4751	15.784	0.0634	7.4987	0.1334
12	2.2522	0.4440	17.888	0.0559	7.9427	0.1259
13	2.4098	0.4150	20.141	0.0497	8.3577	0.1197
14	2.5785	0.3878	22.550	0.0443	8.7455	0.1143
15	2.7590	0.3624	25.129	0.0398	9.1079	0.1098
16	2.9522	0.3387	27.888	0.0359	9.4466	0.1059
17	3.1588	0.3166	30.840	0.0324	9.7632	0.1024
18	3.3799	0.2959	33.999	0.0294	10.059	0.0994
19	3.6165	0.2765	37.379	0.0268	10.336	0.0968
20	3.8697	0.2584	40.995	0.0244	10.594	0.0944
21	4.1406	0.2415	44.865	0.0223	10.836	0.0923
22	4.4304	0.2257	49.006	0.0204	11.061	0.0904
23	4.7405	0.2109	53.436	0.0187	11.272	0.0887
24	5.0724	0.1971	58.177	0.0172	11.469	0.0872
25	5.4274	0.1842	63.249	0.0158	11.654	0.0858
26	5.8074	0.1722	68.676	0.0146	11.826	0.0846
27	6.2139	0.1609	74.484	0.0134	11.987	0.0834
28	6.6488	0.1504	80.698	0.0124	12.137	0.0824
29	7.1143	0.1406	87.347	0.0114	12.278	0.0814
30	7.6123	0.1314	94.461	0.0106	12.409	0.0806

$$i = 8\%$$

n	caf $(1+i)^n$	pwf $\dfrac{1}{(1+i)^n}$	uscaf $\dfrac{(1+i)^n-1}{i}$	ussff $\dfrac{1}{(1+i)^n-1}$	uspwf $\dfrac{(1+i)^n-1}{i(1+i)^n}$	uscrf $\dfrac{i(1+i)^n}{(1+i)^n-1}$
1	1.0800	0.9259	1.0000	1.0000	0.9259	1.0800
2	1.1664	0.8573	2.0800	0.4808	1.7833	0.5608
3	1.2597	0.7938	3.2464	0.3080	2.5771	0.3880
4	1.3605	0.7350	4.5061	0.2219	3.3121	0.3019
5	1.4693	0.6806	5.8666	0.1705	3.9927	0.2505
6	1.5869	0.6302	7.3359	0.1363	4.6229	0.2163
7	1.7138	0.5835	8.9228	0.1121	5.2064	0.1921
8	1.8509	0.5403	10.637	0.0940	5.7466	0.1740
9	1.9990	0.5002	12.488	0.0801	6.2469	0.1601
10	2.1589	0.4632	14.487	0.0690	6.7101	0.1490
11	2.3316	0.4289	16.645	0.0601	7.1390	0.1401
12	2.5182	0.3971	18.977	0.0527	7.5361	0.1327
13	2.7196	0.3677	21.495	0.0465	7.9038	0.1265
14	2.9372	0.3405	24.215	0.0413	8.2442	0.1213
15	3.1722	0.3152	27.152	0.0368	8.5595	0.1168
16	3.4259	0.2919	30.324	0.0330	8.8514	0.1130
17	3.7000	0.2703	33.750	0.0296	9.1216	0.1096
18	3.9960	0.2502	37.450	0.0267	9.3719	0.1067
19	4.3157	0.2317	41.446	0.0241	9.6036	0.1041
20	4.6610	0.2145	45.762	0.0219	9.8181	0.1019
21	5.0338	0.1987	50.423	0.0198	10.017	0.0998
22	5.4365	0.1839	55.457	0.0180	10.201	0.0980
23	5.8715	0.1703	60.893	0.0164	10.371	0.0964
24	6.3412	0.1577	66.765	0.0150	10.529	0.0950
25	6.8485	0.1460	73.106	0.0137	10.675	0.0937
26	7.3964	0.1352	79.954	0.0125	10.810	0.0925
27	7.9881	0.1252	87.351	0.0114	10.935	0.0914
28	8.6271	0.1159	95.339	0.0105	11.051	0.0905
29	9.3173	0.1073	103.97	0.0096	11.158	0.0896
30	10.063	0.0994	113.28	0.0088	11.258	0.0888

$$i = 9\%$$

n	caf $(1 + i)^n$	pwf $\dfrac{1}{(1+i)^n}$	uscaf $\dfrac{(1+i)^n - 1}{i}$	ussff $\dfrac{1}{(1+i)^n - 1}$	uspwf $\dfrac{(1+i)^n - 1}{i(1+i)^n}$	uscrf $\dfrac{i(1+i)^n}{(1+i)^n - 1}$
1	1.0900	0.9174	1.0000	1.0000	0.9174	1.0900
2	1.1881	0.8417	2.0900	0.4785	1.7591	0.5685
3	1.2950	0.7722	3.2781	0.3051	2.5313	0.3951
4	1.4116	0.7084	4.5731	0.2187	3.2397	0.3087
5	1.5386	0.6499	5.9847	0.1671	3.8897	0.2571
6	1.6771	0.5963	7.5233	0.1329	4.4859	0.2229
7	1.8280	0.5470	9.2004	0.1087	5.0330	0.1987
8	1.9926	0.5019	11.028	0.0907	5.5348	0.1807
9	2.1719	0.4604	13.021	0.0768	5.9952	0.1668
10	2.3674	0.4224	15.193	0.0658	6.4177	0.1558
11	2.5804	0.3875	17.560	0.0569	6.8052	0.1469
12	2.8127	0.3555	20.141	0.0497	7.1607	0.1397
13	3.0658	0.3262	22.953	0.0436	7.4869	0.1336
14	3.3417	0.2992	26.019	0.0384	7.7862	0.1284
15	3.6425	0.2745	29.361	0.0341	8.0607	0.1241
16	3.9703	0.2519	33.003	0.0303	8.3126	0.1203
17	4.3276	0.2311	36.974	0.0270	8.5436	0.1170
18	4.7171	0.2120	41.301	0.0242	8.7556	0.1142
19	5.1417	0.1945	46.018	0.0217	8.9501	0.1117
20	5.6044	0.1784	51.160	0.0195	9.1285	0.1095
21	6.1088	0.1637	56.765	0.0176	9.2922	0.1076
22	6.6586	0.1502	62.873	0.0159	9.4424	0.1059
23	7.2579	0.1378	69.532	0.0144	9.5802	0.1044
24	7.9111	0.1264	76.790	0.0130	9.7066	0.1030
25	8.6231	0.1160	84.701	0.0118	9.8226	0.1018
26	9.3992	0.1064	93.324	0.0107	9.9290	0.1007
27	10.245	0.0976	102.72	0.0097	10.027	0.0997
28	11.167	0.0895	112.97	0.0089	10.116	0.0989
29	12.172	0.0822	124.14	0.0081	10.198	0.0981
30	13.268	0.0754	136.31	0.0073	10.274	0.0973

$$i = 10\%$$

n	caf $(1 + i)^n$	pwf $\dfrac{1}{(1+i)^n}$	uscaf $\dfrac{(1+i)^n - 1}{i}$	ussff $\dfrac{1}{(1+i)^n - 1}$	uspwf $\dfrac{(1+i)^n - 1}{i(1+i)^n}$	uscrf $\dfrac{i(1+i)^n}{(1+i)^n - 1}$
1	1.1000	0.9091	1.0000	1.0000	0.9091	1.1000
2	1.2100	0.8264	2.1000	0.4762	1.7355	0.5762
3	1.3310	0.7513	3.3100	0.3021	2.4869	0.4021
4	1.4641	0.6830	4.6410	0.2155	3.1699	0.3155
5	1.6105	0.6209	6.1051	0.1638	3.7908	0.2638
6	1.7716	0.5645	7.7156	0.1296	4.3553	0.2296
7	1.9487	0.5132	9.4872	0.1054	4.8684	0.2054
8	2.1436	0.4665	11.436	0.0874	5.3349	0.1874
9	2.3579	0.4241	13.579	0.0736	5.7590	0.1736
10	2.5937	0.3855	15.937	0.0627	6.1446	0.1627
11	2.8531	0.3505	18.531	0.0540	6.4951	0.1540
12	3.1384	0.3186	21.384	0.0468	6.8137	0.1468
13	3.4523	0.2897	24.523	0.0408	7.1034	0.1408
14	3.7975	0.2633	27.975	0.0357	7.3667	0.1357
15	4.1772	0.2394	31.772	0.0315	7.6061	0.1315
16	4.5950	0.2176	35.950	0.0278	7.8237	0.1278
17	5.0545	0.1978	40.545	0.0247	8.0216	0.1247
18	5.5599	0.1799	45.599	0.0219	8.2014	0.1219
19	6.1159	0.1635	51.159	0.0195	8.3649	0.1195
20	6.7275	0.1486	57.275	0.0175	8.5136	0.1175
21	7.4002	0.1351	64.002	0.0156	8.6487	0.1156
22	8.1403	0.1228	71.403	0.0140	8.7715	0.1140
23	8.9543	0.1117	79.543	0.0126	8.8832	0.1126
24	9.8497	0.1015	88.497	0.0113	8.9847	0.1113
25	10.835	0.0923	98.347	0.0102	9.0770	0.1102
26	11.918	0.0839	109.18	0.0092	9.1609	0.1092
27	13.110	0.0763	121.10	0.0083	9.2372	0.1083
28	14.421	0.0693	134.21	0.0075	9.3066	0.1075
29	15.863	0.0630	148.63	0.0067	9.3696	0.1067
30	17.449	0.0573	164.49	0.0061	9.4269	0.1061

$$i = 11\%$$

n	caf $(1 + i)^n$	pwf $\dfrac{1}{(1+i)^n}$	uscaf $\dfrac{(1+i)^n-1}{i}$	ussff $\dfrac{1}{(1+i)^n-1}$	uspwf $\dfrac{(1+i)^n-1}{i(1+i)^n}$	uscrf $\dfrac{i(1+i)^n}{(1+i)^n-1}$
1	1.1100	0.9009	1.0000	1.0000	0.9009	1.1100
2	1.2321	0.8116	2.1100	0.4739	1.7125	0.5839
3	1.3676	0.7312	3.3421	0.2992	2.4437	0.4092
4	1.5181	0.6587	4.7097	0.2123	3.1024	0.3223
5	1.6851	0.5935	6.2278	0.1606	3.6959	0.2706
6	1.8704	0.5346	7.9129	0.1264	4.2305	0.2364
7	2.0762	0.4817	9.7833	0.1022	4.7122	0.2122
8	2.3045	0.4339	11.859	0.0843	5.1461	0.1943
9	2.5580	0.3909	14.164	0.0706	5.5370	0.1806
10	2.8394	0.3522	16.722	0.0598	5.8892	0.1698
11	3.1518	0.3173	19.561	0.0511	6.2065	0.1611
12	3.4985	0.2858	22.713	0.0440	6.4924	0.1540
13	3.8833	0.2575	26.212	0.0382	6.7499	0.1482
14	4.3104	0.2320	30.095	0.0332	6.9819	0.1432
15	4.7846	0.2090	34.405	0.0291	7.1909	0.1391
16	5.3109	0.1883	39.190	0.0255	7.3792	0.1355
17	5.8951	0.1696	44.501	0.0225	7.5488	0.1325
18	6.5436	0.1528	50.396	0.0198	7.7016	0.1298
19	7.2633	0.1377	56.939	0.0176	7.8393	0.1276
20	8.0623	0.1240	64.203	0.0156	7.9633	0.1256
21	8.9492	0.1117	72.265	0.0138	8.0751	0.1238
22	9.9336	0.1007	81.214	0.0123	8.1757	0.1223
23	11.026	0.0907	91.148	0.0110	8.2664	0.1210
24	12.239	0.0817	102.17	0.0098	8.3481	0.1198
25	13.585	0.0736	114.41	0.0087	8.4217	0.1187
26	15.080	0.0663	128.00	0.0078	8.4881	0.1178
27	16.739	0.0597	143.08	0.0070	8.5478	0.1170
28	18.580	0.0538	159.82	0.0063	8.6016	0.1163
29	20.624	0.0485	178.40	0.0056	8.6501	0.1156
30	22.892	0.0437	199.02	0.0050	8.6938	0.1150

$$i = 12\%$$

n	caf $(1+i)^n$	pwf $\dfrac{1}{(1+i)^n}$	uscaf $\dfrac{(1+i)^n-1}{i}$	ussff $\dfrac{1}{(1+i)^n-1}$	uspwf $\dfrac{(1+i)^n-1}{i(1+i)^n}$	uscrf $\dfrac{i(1+i)^n}{(1+i)^n-1}$
1	1.1200	0.8929	1.0000	1.0000	0.8929	1.1200
2	1.2544	0.7972	2.1200	0.4717	1.6901	0.5917
3	1.4049	0.7118	3.3744	0.2963	2.4018	0.4163
4	1.5735	0.6355	4.7793	0.2092	3.0373	0.3292
5	1.7623	0.5674	6.3528	0.1574	3.6048	0.2774
6	1.9738	0.5066	8.1152	0.1232	4.1114	0.2432
7	2.2107	0.4523	10.089	0.0991	4.5638	0.2191
8	2.4760	0.4039	12.300	0.0813	4.9676	0.2013
9	2.7731	0.3606	14.776	0.0677	5.3282	0.1877
10	3.1058	0.3220	17.549	0.0570	5.6502	0.1770
11	3.4785	0.2875	20.655	0.0484	5.9377	0.1684
12	3.8960	0.2567	24.133	0.0414	6.1944	0.1614
13	4.3635	0.2292	28.029	0.0357	6.4235	0.1557
14	4.8871	0.2046	32.393	0.0309	6.6282	0.1509
15	5.4736	0.1827	37.280	0.0268	6.8109	0.1468
16	6.1304	0.1631	42.753	0.0234	6.9740	0.1434
17	6.8660	0.1456	48.884	0.0205	7.1196	0.1405
18	7.6900	0.1300	55.750	0.0179	7.2497	0.1379
19	8.6128	0.1161	63.440	0.0158	7.3658	0.1358
20	9.6463	0.1037	72.052	0.0139	7.4694	0.1339
21	10.804	0.0926	81.699	0.0122	7.5620	0.1322
22	12.100	0.0826	92.503	0.0108	7.6446	0.1308
23	13.552	0.0738	104.60	0.0096	7.7184	0.1296
24	15.179	0.0659	118.16	0.0085	7.7843	0.1285
25	17.000	0.0588	133.33	0.0075	7.8431	0.1275
26	19.040	0.0525	150.33	0.0067	7.8957	0.1267
27	21.325	0.0469	169:37	0.0059	7.9426	0.1259
28	23.884	0.0419	190.70	0.0052	7.9844	0.1252
29	26.750	0.0374	214.58	0.0047	8.0218	0.1247
30	29.960	0.0334	241.33	0.0041	8.0552	0.1241

$$i = 13\%$$

n	caf $(1+i)^n$	pwf $\dfrac{1}{(1+i)^n}$	uscaf $\dfrac{(1+i)^n-1}{i}$	ussff $\dfrac{1}{(1+i)^n-1}$	uspwf $\dfrac{(1+i)^n-1}{i(1+i)^n}$	uscrf $\dfrac{i(1+i)^n}{(1+i)^n-1}$
1	1.1300	0.8850	1.0000	1.0000	0.8850	1.1300
2	1.2769	0.7831	2.1300	0.4695	1.6681	0.5995
3	1.4429	0.6931	3.4069	0.2935	2.3612	0.4235
4	1.6305	0.6133	4.8498	0.2062	2.9745	0.3362
5	1.8424	0.5428	6.4803	0.1543	3.5172	0.2843
6	2.0820	0.4803	8.3227	0.1202	3.9975	0.2502
7	2.3526	0.4251	10.405	0.0961	4.4226	0.2261
8	2.6584	0.3762	12.757	0.0784	4.7988	0.2084
9	3.0040	0.3329	15.416	0.0649	5.1317	0.1949
10	3.3946	0.2946	18.420	0.0543	5.4262	0.1843
11	3.8359	0.2607	21.814	0.0458	5.6869	0.1758
12	4.3345	0.2307	25.650	0.0390	5.9176	0.1690
13	4.8980	0.2042	29.985	0.0334	6.1218	0.1634
14	5.5348	0.1807	34.883	0.0287	6.3025	0.1587
15	6.2543	0.1599	40.417	0.0247	6.4624	0.1547
16	7.0673	0.1415	46.672	0.0214	6.6039	0.1514
17	7.9861	0.1252	53.739	0.0186	6.7291	0.1486
18	9.0243	0.1108	61.725	0.0162	6.8399	0.1462
19	10.197	0.0981	70.749	0.0141	6.9380	0.1441
20	11.523	0.0868	80.947	0.0124	7.0248	0.1424
21	13.021	0.0768	92.470	0.0108	7.1016	0.1408
22	14.714	0.0680	105.49	0.0095	7.1695	0.1395
23	16.627	0.0601	120.20	0.0083	7.2297	0.1383
24	18.788	0.0532	136.83	0.0073	7.2829	0.1373
25	21.231	0.0471	155.62	0.0064	7.3300	0.1364
26	23.991	0.0417	176.85	0.0057	7.3717	0.1357
27	27.109	0.0369	200.84	0.0050	7.4086	0.1350
28	30.633	0.0326	227.95	0.0044	7.4412	0.1344
29	34.616	0.0289	258.58	0.0039	7.4701	0.1339
30	39.116	0.0256	293.20	0.0034	7.4957	0.1334

$$i = 14\%$$

n	caf $(1+i)^n$	pwf $\dfrac{1}{(1+i)^n}$	uscaf $\dfrac{(1+i)^n-1}{i}$	ussff $\dfrac{1}{(1+i)^n-1}$	uspwf $\dfrac{(1+i)^n-1}{i(1+i)^n}$	uscrf $\dfrac{i(1+i)^n}{(1+i)^n-1}$
1	1.1400	0.8772	1.0000	1.0000	0.8772	1.1400
2	1.2996	0.7695	2.1400	0.4673	1.6467	0.6073
3	1.4815	0.6750	3.4396	0.2907	2.3216	0.4307
4	1.6890	0.5921	4.9211	0.2032	2.9137	0.3432
5	1.9254	0.5194	6.6101	0.1513	3.4331	0.2913
6	2.1950	0.4556	8.5355	0.1172	3.8887	0.2572
7	2.5023	0.3996	10.730	0.0932	4.2883	0.2332
8	2.8526	0.3506	13.233	0.0756	4.6389	0.2156
9	3.2519	0.3075	16.085	0.0622	4.9464	0.2022
10	3.7072	0.2697	19.337	0.0517	5.2161	0.1917
11	4.2262	0.2366	23.045	0.0434	5.4527	0.1834
12	4.8179	0.2076	27.271	0.0367	5.6603	0.1767
13	5.4924	0.1821	32.089	0.0312	5.8424	0.1712
14	6.2613	0.1597	37.581	0.0266	6.0021	0.1666
15	7.1379	0.1401	43.482	0.0228	6.1422	0.1628
16	8.1372	0.1229	50.980	0.0196	6.2651	0.1596
17	9.2765	0.1078	59.118	0.0169	6.3729	0.1569
18	10.575	0.0946	68.394	0.0146	6.4674	0.1546
19	12.056	0.0829	78.969	0.0127	6.5504	0.1527
20	13.743	0.0728	91.025	0.0110	6.6231	0.1510
21	15.668	0.0638	104.77	0.0095	6.6870	0.1495
22	17.861	0.0560	120.44	0.0083	6.7429	0.1483
23	20.362	0.0491	138.30	0.0072	6.7921	0.1472
24	23.212	0.0431	158.66	0.0063	6.8351	0.1463
25	26.462	0.0378	181.87	0.0055	6.8729	0.1455
26	30.167	0.0331	208.33	0.0048	6.9061	0.1448
27	34.390	0.0291	238.50	0.0042	6.9352	0.1442
28	39.204	0.0255	272.89	0.0037	6.9607	0.1437
29	44.693	0.0224	312.09	0.0032	6.9830	0.1432
30	50.950	0.0196	356.79	0.0028	7.0027	0.1428

$$i = 15\%$$

	caf	pwf	uscaf	ussff	uspwf	uscrf
n	$(1+i)^n$	$\dfrac{1}{(1+i)^n}$	$\dfrac{(1+i)^n-1}{i}$	$\dfrac{1}{(1+i)^n-1}$	$\dfrac{(1+i)^n-1}{i(1+i)^n}$	$\dfrac{i(1+i)^n}{(1+i)^n-1}$
1	1.1500	0.8696	1.0000	1.0000	0.8696	1.1500
2	1.3225	0.7561	2.1500	0.4651	1.6257	0.6151
3	1.5209	0.6575	3.4725	0.2880	2.2832	0.4380
4	1.7490	0.5718	4.9934	0.2003	2.8550	0.3503
5	2.0114	0.4972	6.7424	0.1483	3.3522	0.2983
6	2.3131	0.4323	8.7537	0.1142	3.7845	0.2642
7	2.6600	0.3759	11.067	0.0904	4.1604	0.2404
8	3.0590	0.3269	13.727	0.0729	4.4873	0.2229
9	3.5179	0.2843	16.786	0.0596	4.7716	0.2096
10	4.0456	0.2472	20.304	0.0493	5.0188	0.1993
11	4.6524	0.2149	24.349	0.0411	5.2337	0.1911
12	5.3503	0.1869	29.002	0.0345	5.4206	0.1845
13	6.1528	0.1625	34.352	0.0291	5.5831	0.1791
14	7.0757	0.1413	40.505	0.0247	5.7245	0.1747
15	8.1371	0.1229	47.580	0.0210	5.8474	0.1710
16	9.3576	0.1069	55.717	0.0179	5.9542	0.1679
17	10.761	0.0929	65.075	0.0154	6.0472	0.1654
18	12.375	0.0808	75.836	0.0132	6.1280	0.1632
19	14.232	0.0703	88.212	0.0113	6.1982	0.1613
20	16.367	0.0611	102.44	0.0098	6.2593	0.1598
21	18.822	0.0531	118.81	0.0084	6.3125	0.1584
22	21.645	0.0462	137.63	0.0073	6.3587	0.1573
23	24.891	0.0402	159.28	0.0063	6.3988	0.1563
24	28.625	0.0349	184.17	0.0054	6.4338	0.1554
25	32.919	0.0304	212.79	0.0047	6.4641	0.1547
26	37.857	0.0264	245.71	0;0041	6.4906	0.1541
27	43.535	0.0230	283.57	0.0035	6.5135	0.1535
28	50.066	0.0200	327.10	0.0031	6.5335	0.1531
29	57.575	0.0174	377.17	0.0027	6.5509	0.1527
30	66.212	0.0151	434.75	0.0023	6.5660	0.1523

$$i = 16\%$$

	caf	pwf	uscaf	ussff	uspwf	uscrf
n	$(1+i)^n$	$\dfrac{1}{(1+i)^n}$	$\dfrac{(1+i)^n-1}{i}$	$\dfrac{1}{(1+i)^n-1}$	$\dfrac{(1+i)^n-1}{i(1+i)^n}$	$\dfrac{i(1+i)^n}{(1+i)^n-1}$
1	1.1600	0.8621	1.0000	1.0000	0.8621	1.1600
2	1.3456	0.7432	2.1600	0.4630	1.6052	0.6230
3	1.5609	0.6407	3.5056	0.2853	2.2459	0.4453
4	1.8106	0.5523	5.0665	0.1974	2.7982	0.3574
5	2.1003	0.4761	6.8771	0.1454	3.2743	0.3054
6	2.4364	0.4104	8.9775	0.1114	3.6847	0.2714
7	2.8262	0.3538	11.414	0.0876	4.0386	0.2476
8	3.2784	0.3050	14.240	0.0702	4.3436	0.2302
9	3.8030	0.2630	17.519	0.0571	4.6065	0.2171
10	4.4114	0.2267	21.321	0.0469	4.8332	0.2069
11	5.1173	0.1954	25.733	0.0389	5.0286	0.1989
12	5.9360	0.1685	30.850	0.0324	5.1971	0.1924
13	6.8858	0.1452	36.786	0.0272	5.3423	0.1872
14	7.9875	0.1252	43.672	0.0229	5.4675	0.1829
15	9.2655	0.1079	51.660	0.0194	5.5755	0.1794
16	10.748	0.0930	60.925	0.0164	5.6685	0.1764
17	12.468	0.0802	71.673	0.0140	5.7487	0.1740
18	14.463	0.0691	84.141	0.0119	5.8178	0.1719
19	16.777	0.0596	98.603	0.0101	5.8775	0.1700
20	19.461	0.0514	115.38	0.0087	5.9288	0.1687
21	22.574	0.0443	134.84	0.0074	5.9731	0.1674
22	26.186	0.0382	157.41	0.0064	6.0113	0.1664
23	30.376	0.0329	183.60	0.0054	6.0442	0.1654
24	35.236	0.0284	213.98	0.0047	6.0726	0.1647
25	40.874	0.0245	249.21	0.0040	6.0971	0.1640
26	47.414	0.0211	290.09	0.0034	6.1182	0.1634
27	55.000	0.0182	337.50	0.0030	6.1364	0.1630
28	63.800	0.0157	392.50	0.0025	6.1520	0.1625
29	74.009	0.0135	456.30	0.0022	6.1656	0.1622
30	85.850	0.0116	530.31	0.0019	6.1772	0.1619

$$i = 17\%$$

n	caf $(1+i)^n$	pwf $\dfrac{1}{(1+i)^n}$	uscaf $\dfrac{(1+i)^n-1}{i}$	ussff $\dfrac{1}{(1+i)^n-1}$	uspwf $\dfrac{(1+i)^n-1}{i(1+i)^n}$	uscrf $\dfrac{i(1+i)^n}{(1+i)^n-1}$
1	1.1700	0.8547	1.0000	1.0000	0.8547	1.1700
2	1.3689	0.7305	2.1700	0.4608	1.5852	0.6308
3	1.6016	0.6244	3.5389	0.2826	2.2096	0.4526
4	1.8739	0.5337	5.1405	0.1945	2.7432	0.3645
5	2.1924	0.4561	7.0144	0.1426	3.1993	0.3126
6	2.5652	0.3898	9.2068	0.1086	3.5892	0.2786
7	3.0012	0.3332	11.772	0.0849	3.9224	0.2549
8	3.5115	0.2848	14.773	0.0677	4.2072	0.2377
9	4.1084	0.2434	18.285	0.0547	4.4506	0.2247
10	4.8068	0.2080	22.393	0.0447	4.6586	0.2147
11	5.6240	0.1778	27.200	0.0368	4.8364	0.2068
12	6.5801	0.1520	32.824	0.0305	4.9884	0.2005
13	7.6987	0.1299	39.404	0.0254	5.1183	0.1954
14	9.0075	0.1110	47.103	0.0212	5.2293	0.1912
15	10.539	0.0949	56.110	0.0178	5.3242	0.1878
16	12.330	0.0811	66.649	0.0150	5.4053	0.1850
17	14.426	0.0693	78.979	0.0127	5.4746	0.1827
18	16.879	0.0592	93.406	0.0107	5.5339	0.1807
19	19.748	0.0506	110.28	0.0091	5.5845	0.1791
20	23.106	0.0433	130.03	0.0077	5.6278	0.1777
21	27.034	0.0370	153.14	0.0065	5.6648	0.1765
22	31.629	0.0316	180.17	0.0056	5.6964	0.1756
23	37.006	0.0270	211.80	0.0047	5.7234	0.1747
24	43.297	0.0231	248.81	0.0040	5.7465	0.1740
25	50.658	0.0197	292.10	0.0034	5.7662	0.1734
26	59.270	0.0169	342.76	0.0029	5.7831	0.1729
27	69.345	0.0144	402.03	0.0025	5.7975	0.1725
28	81.134	0.0123	471.38	0.0021	5.8099	0.1721
29	94.927	0.0105	552.51	0.0018	5.8204	0.1718
30	111.06	0.0090	647.44	0.0015	5.8294	0.1715

$$i = 18\%$$

n	caf $(1 + i)^n$	pwf $\dfrac{1}{(1+i)^n}$	uscaf $\dfrac{(1+i)^n - 1}{i}$	ussff $\dfrac{1}{(1+i)^n - 1}$	uspwf $\dfrac{(1+i)^n - 1}{i(1+i)^n}$	uscrf $\dfrac{i(1+i)^n}{(1+i)^n - 1}$
1	1.1800	0.8475	1.0000	1.0000	0.8475	1.1800
2	1.3924	0.7182	2.1800	0.4587	1.5656	0.6387
3	1.6430	0.6086	3.5724	0.2799	2.1743	0.4599
4	1.9388	0.5158	5.2154	0.1917	2.6901	0.3717
5	2.2878	0.4371	7.1542	0.1398	3.1272	0.3198
6	2.6996	0.3704	9.4420	0.1059	3.4976	0.2859
7	3.1855	0.3139	12.142	0.0824	3.8115	0.2624
8	3.7589	0.2660	15.327	0.0652	4.0776	0.2452
9	4.4355	0.2255	19.086	0.0524	4.3030	0.2324
10	5.2338	0.1911	23.521	0.0425	4.4941	0.2225
11	6.1759	0.1619	28.755	0.0348	4.6560	0.2148
12	7.2876	0.1372	34.931	0.0286	4.7932	0.2086
13	8.5994	0.1163	42.219	0.0237	4.9095	0.2037
14	10.147	0.0985	50.818	0.0197	5.0081	0.1997
15	11.974	0.0835	60.965	0.0164	5.0916	0.1964
16	14.129	0.0708	72.939	0.0137	5.1624	0.1937
17	16.672	0.0600	87.068	0.0115	5.2223	0.1915
18	19.673	0.0508	103.74	0.0096	5.2732	0.1896
19	23.214	0.0431	123.41	0.0081	5.3162	0.1881
20	27.393	0.0365	146.63	0.0068	5.3527	0.1868
21	32.324	0.0309	174.02	0.0057	5.3837	0.1857
22	38.142	0.0262	206.34	0.0048	5.4009	0.1848
23	45.008	0.0222	244.49	0.0041	5.4321	0.1841
24	53.109	0.0188	289.49	0.0035	5.4509	0.1835
25	62.669	0.0160	342.60	0.0029	5.4669	0.1829
26	73.949	0.0135	405.27	0.0025	5.4804	0.1825
27	87.260	0.0115	479.22	0.0021	5.4919	0.1821
28	102.97	0.0097	566.48	0.0018	5.5016	0.1818
29	121.50	0.0082	669.45	0.0015	5.5098	0.1815
30	143.37	0.0070	790.95	0.0013	5.5168	0.1813

$$i = 19\%$$

n	caf $(1+i)^n$	pwf $\dfrac{1}{(1+i)^n}$	uscaf $\dfrac{(1+i)^n-1}{i}$	ussff $\dfrac{1}{(1+i)^n-1}$	uspwf $\dfrac{(1+i)^n-1}{i(1+i)^n}$	uscrf $\dfrac{i(1+i)^n}{(1+i)^n-1}$
1	1.1900	0.8403	1.0000	1.0000	0.8403	1.1900
2	1.4161	0.7062	2.1900	0.4566	1.5465	0.6466
3	1.6852	0.5934	3.6061	0.2773	2.1399	0.4673
4	2.0053	0.4987	5.2913	0.1890	2.6386	0.3790
5	2.3864	0.4190	7.2966	0.1371	3.0576	0.3271
6	2.8398	0.3521	9.6830	0.1033	3.4098	0.2933
7	3.3793	0.2959	12.523	0.0799	3.7057	0.2699
8	4.0214	0.2487	15.902	0.0629	3.9544	0.2529
9	4.7854	0.2090	19.923	0.0502	4.1633	0.2402
10	5.6947	0.1756	24.709	0.0405	4.3389	0.2305
11	6.7767	0.1476	30.404	0.0329	4.4865	0.2229
12	8.0642	0.1240	37.180	0.0269	4.6105	0.2169
13	9.5964	0.1042	45.244	0.0221	4.7147	0.2121
14	11.420	0.0876	54.841	0.0182	4.8023	0.2082
15	13.590	0.0736	66.261	0.0151	4.8759	0.2051
16	16.172	0.0618	79.850	0.0125	4.9377	0.2025
17	19.244	0.0520	96.022	0.0104	4.9897	0.2004
18	22.901	0.0437	115.27	0.0087	5.0333	0.1987
19	27.252	0.0367	138.17	0.0072	5.0700	0.1972
20	32.429	0.0308	165.42	0.0060	5.1009	0.1960
21	38.591	0.0259	197.85	0.0051	5.1268	0.1951
22	45.923	0.0218	236.44	0.0042	5.1486	0.1942
23	54.649	0.0183	282.36	0.0035	5.1668	0.1935
24	65.032	0.0154	337.01	0.0030	5.1822	0.1930
25	77.388	0.0129	402.04	0.0025	5.1951	0.1925
26	92.092	0.0109	479.43	0.0021	5.2060	0.1921
27	109.59	0.0091	571.52	0.0017	5.2151	0.1917
28	130.41	0.0077	681.11	0.0015	5.2228	0.1915
29	155.19	0.0064	811.52	0.0012	5.2292	0.1912
30	184.68	0.0054	966.71	0.0010	5.2347	0.1910

$$i = 20\%$$

	caf	pwf	uscaf	ussff	uspwf	uscrf
n	$(1+i)^n$	$\dfrac{1}{(1+i)^n}$	$\dfrac{(1+i)^n-1}{i}$	$\dfrac{1}{(1+i)^n-1}$	$\dfrac{(1+i)^n-1}{i(1+i)^n}$	$\dfrac{i(1+i)^n}{(1+i)^n-1}$
1	1.2000	0.8333	1.0000	1.0000	0.8333	1.2000
2	1.4400	0.6944	2.2000	0.4545	1.5278	0.6545
3	1.7280	0.5787	3.6400	0.2747	2.1065	0.4747
4	2.0736	0.4823	5.3680	0.1863	2.5887	0.3863
5	2.4883	0.4019	7.4416	0.1344	2.9906	0.3344
6	2.9860	0.3349	9.9299	0.1007	3.3255	0.3007
7	3.5832	0.2791	12.916	0.0774	3.6046	0.2774
8	4.2998	0.2326	16.499	0.0606	3.8372	0.2606
9	5.1598	0.1938	20.799	0.0481	4.0310	0.2481
10	6.1917	0.1615	25.959	0.0385	4.1925	0.2385
11	7.4301	0.1346	32.150	0.0311	4.3271	0.2311
12	8.9161	0.1122	39.581	0.0253	4.4392	0.2253
13	10.699	0.0935	48.497	0.0206	4.5327	0.2206
14	12.839	0.0779	59.196	0.0169	4.6106	0.2169
15	15.407	0.0649	72.035	0.0139	4.6755	0.2139
16	18.488	0.0541	87.442	0.0114	4.7296	0.2114
17	22.186	0.0451	105.93	0.0094	4.7746	0.2094
18	26.623	0.0376	128.12	0.0078	4.8122	0.2078
19	31.948	0.0313	154.74	0.0065	4.8435	0.2065
20	38.338	0.0261	186.69	0.0054	4.8696	0.2054
21	46.005	0.0217	225.03	0.0044	4.8913	0.2044
22	55.206	0.0181	271.03	0.0037	4.9094	0.2037
23	66.247	0.0151	326.24	0.0031	4.9245	0.2031
24	79.497	0.0126	392.48	0.0025	4.9371	0.2025
25	95.396	0.0105	471.98	0.0021	4.9476	0.2021
26	114.48	0.0087	567.38	0.0018	4.9563	0.2018
27	137.37	0.0073	681.85	0.0015	4.9636	0.2015
28	164.84	0.0061	819.22	0.0012	4.9697	0.2012
29	197.81	0.0051	984.07	0.0010	4.9747	0.2010
30	237.38	0.0042	1181.90	0.0008	4.9789	0.2008

$$i = 21\%$$

n	caf $(1+i)^n$	pwf $\dfrac{1}{(1+i)^n}$	uscaf $\dfrac{(1+i)^n-1}{i}$	ussff $\dfrac{1}{(1+i)^n-1}$	uspwf $\dfrac{(1+i)^n-1}{i(1+i)^n}$	uscrf $\dfrac{i(1+i)^n}{(1+i)^n-1}$
1	1.2100	0.8264	1.0000	1.0000	0.8264	1.2100
2	1.4641	0.6830	2.2100	0.4525	1.5095	0.6625
3	1.7716	0.5645	3.6741	0.2722	2.0739	0.4822
4	2.1436	0.4665	5.4457	0.1836	2.5404	0.3936
5	2.5937	0.3855	7.5892	0.1318	2.9260	0.3418
6	3.1384	0.3186	10.183	0.0982	3.2446	0.3082
7	3.7975	0.2633	13.321	0.0751	3.5079	0.2851
8	4.5950	0.2176	17.119	0.0584	3.7256	0.2684
9	5.5599	0.1799	21.714	0.0461	3.9054	0.2561
10	6.7275	0.1486	27.274	0.0367	4.0541	0.2467
11	8.1403	0.1228	34.001	0.0294	4.1769	0.2394
12	9.8497	0.1015	41.142	0.0237	4.2784	0.2337
13	11.918	0.0839	51.991	0.0192	4.3624	0.2292
14	14.421	0.0693	63.909	0.0156	4.4317	0.2256
15	17.449	0.0573	78.330	0.0128	4.4890	0.2228
16	21.114	0.0474	95.780	0.0104	4.5364	0.2204
17	25.548	0.0391	116.89	0.0086	4.5755	0.2186
18	30.913	0.0323	142.44	0.0070	4.6079	0.2170
19	37.404	0.0267	173.35	0.0058	4.6346	0.2158
20	45.259	0.0221	210.76	0.0047	4.6567	0.2147
21	54.764	0.0183	256.02	0.0039	4.6750	0.2139
22	66.264	0.0151	310.78	0.0032	4.6900	0.2132
23	80.180	0.0125	377.05	0.0027	4.7025	0.2127
24	97.017	0.0103	457.22	0.0022	4.7128	0.2122
25	117.39	0.0085	554.24	0.0018	4.7213	0.2118
26	142.04	0.0070	671.63	0;0015	4.7284	0.2115
27	171.87	0.0058	813.68	0.0012	4.7342	0.2112
28	207.97	0.0048	985.55	0.0010	4.7390	0.2110
29	251.64	0.0040	1193.50	0.0008	4.7430	0.2108
30	304.48	0.0033	1445.20	0.0007	4.7463	0.2107

$$i = 22\%$$

n	caf $(1+i)^n$	pwf $\dfrac{1}{(1+i)^n}$	uscaf $\dfrac{(1+i)^n-1}{i}$	ussff $\dfrac{1}{(1+i)^n-1}$	uspwf $\dfrac{(1+i)^n-1}{i(1+i)^n}$	uscrf $\dfrac{i(1+i)^n}{(1+i)^n-1}$
1	1.2200	0.8197	1.0000	1.0000	0.8197	1.2200
2	1.4884	0.6719	2.2200	0.4505	1.4915	0.6705
3	1.8158	0.5507	3.7084	0.2697	2.0422	0.4897
4	2.2153	0.4514	1.5242	0.1810	2.4936	0.4010
5	2.7027	0.3700	7.7396	0.1292	2.8636	0.3492
6	3.2973	0.3033	10.442	0.0958	3.1669	0.3158
7	4.0227	0.2486	13.740	0.0728	3.4155	0.2928
8	4.9077	0.2038	17.762	0.0563	3.6193	0.2763
9	5.9874	0.1670	22.670	0.0441	3.7863	0.2641
10	7.3046	0.1369	28.657	0.0349	3.9232	0.2549
11	8.9117	0.1122	35.962	0.0278	4.0354	0.2478
12	10.872	0.0920	44.874	0.0223	4.1274	0.2423
13	13.264	0.0754	55.746	0.0179	4.2028	0.2379
14	16.182	0.0618	69.010	0.0145	4.2646	0.2345
15	19.742	0.0507	85.192	0.0117	4.3152	0.2317
16	24.086	0.0415	104.93	0.0095	4.3567	0.2295
17	29.384	0.0340	129.02	0.0078	4.3908	0.2278
18	35.849	0.0279	158.40	0.0063	4.4187	0.2263
19	43.736	0.0229	194.25	0.0051	4.4415	0.2251
20	53.358	0.0187	237.99	0.0042	4.4603	0.2242
21	65.096	0.0154	291.35	0.0034	4.4756	0.2234
22	79.418	0.0126	356.44	0.0028	4.4882	0.2228
23	96.889	0.0103	435.86	0.0023	4.4985	0.2223
24	118.21	0.0085	532.75	0.0019	4.5070	0.2219
25	144.21	0.0069	650.96	0.0015	4.5139	0.2215
26	175.94	0.0057	795.17	0.0013	4.5196	0.2213
27	214.64	0.0047	971.10	0.0010	4.5243	0.2210
28	261.86	0.0038	1185.70	0.0008	4.5281	0.2208
29	319.47	0.0031	1447.60	0.0007	4.5312	0.2207
30	389.76	0.0026	1767.10	0.0006	4.5338	0.2206

$$i = 23\%$$

n	caf $(1 + i)^n$	pwf $\dfrac{1}{(1+i)^n}$	uscaf $\dfrac{(1+i)^n-1}{i}$	ussff $\dfrac{1}{(1+i)^n-1}$	uspwf $\dfrac{(1+i)^n-1}{i(1+i)^n}$	uscrf $\dfrac{i(1+i)^n}{(1+i)^n-1}$
1	1.2300	0.8130	1.0000	1.0000	0.8130	1.2300
2	1.5129	0.6610	2.2300	0.4484	1.4740	0.6784
3	1.8609	0.5374	3.7429	0.2672	2.0114	0.4972
4	2.2889	0.4369	5.6038	0.1785	2.4483	0.4085
5	2.8153	0.3552	7.8926	0.1267	2.8035	0.3567
6	3.4628	0.28$8	10.708	0.0934	3.0923	0.3234
7	4.2593	0.2348	14.171	0.0706	3.3270	0.3006
8	5.2389	0.1909	18.430	0.0543	3.5179	0.2843
9	6.4439	0.1552	23.669	0.0422	3.6731	0.2722
10	7.9259	0.1262	30.113	0.0332	3.7993	0.2632
11	9.7489	0.1026	38.039	0.0263	3.9018	0.2563
12	11.991	0.0834	47.788	0.0209	3.9852	0.2509
13	14.749	0.0678	59.779	0.0167	4.0530	0.2467
14	18.141	0.0551	74.528	0.0134	4.1082	0.2434
15	22.314	0.0448	92.669	0.0108	4.1530	0.2408
16	27.446	0.0364	114.98	0.0087	4.1894	0.2387
17	33.759	0.0296	142.43	0.0070	4.2190	0.2370
18	41.523	0.0241	176.19	0.0057	4.2431	0.2357
19	51.074	0.0196	217.71	0.0046	4.2627	0.2346
20	62.821	0.0159	268.79	0.0037	4.2786	0.2337
21	77.269	0.0129	331.61	0.0030	4.2916	0.2330
22	95.041	0.0105	408.88	0.0024	4.3021	0.2324
23	116.90	0.0086	503.92	0.0020	4.3106	0.2320
24	143.79	0.0070	620.82	0.0016	4.3176	0.2316
25	176.86	0.0057	764.61	0.0013	4.3232	0.2313
26	217.54	0.0046	941.46	0.0011	4.3278	0.2311
27	267.57	0.0037	1159.00	0.0009	4.3316	0.2309
28	329.11	0.0030	1426.60	0.0007	4.3346	0.2307
29	404.81	0.0025	1755.70	0.0006	4.3371	0.2306
30	497.91	0.0020	2160.50	0.0005	4.3391	0.2305

$$i = 24\%$$

n	caf $(1+i)^n$	pwf $\dfrac{1}{(1+i)^n}$	uscaf $\dfrac{(1+i)^n-1}{i}$	ussff $\dfrac{1}{(1+i)^n-1}$	uspwf $\dfrac{(1+i)^n-1}{i(1+i)^n}$	uscrf $\dfrac{i(1+i)^n}{(1+i)^n-1}$
1	1.2400	0.8065	1.0000	1.0000	0.8065	1.2400
2	1.5376	0.6504	2.2400	0.4464	1.4568	0.6864
3	1.9066	0.5245	3.7776	0.2647	2.9813	0.5047
4	2.3642	0.4230	5.6842	0.1759	2.4043	0.4159
5	2.9316	0.3411	8.0484	0.1242	2.7454	0.3642
6	3.6352	0.2751	10.980	0.0911	3.0205	0.3311
7	4.5077	0.2218	14.615	0.0684	3.2423	0.3084
8	5.5895	0.1789	19.123	0.0523	3.4212	0.2923
9	6.9310	0.1443	24.712	0.0405	3.5655	0.2805
10	8.5944	0.1164	31.643	0.0316	3.6819	0.2716
11	10.657	0.0938	40.238	0.0249	3.7757	0.2649
12	13.215	0.0757	50.895	0.0196	3.8514	0.2596
13	16.386	0.0610	64.110	0.0156	3.9124	0.2556
14	20.319	0.0492	80.496	0.0124	3.9616	0.2524
15	25.196	0.0397	100.82	0.0099	4.0013	0.2499
16	31.243	0.0320	126.01	0.0079	4.0333	0.2479
17	38.741	0.0258	157.25	0.0064	4.0591	0.2464
18	48.039	0.0208	195.99	0.0051	4.0799	0.2451
19	59.568	0.0168	244.03	0.0041	4.0967	0.2441
20	73.864	0.0135	303.60	0.0033	4.1103	0.2433
21	91.592	0.0109	377.46	0.0026	4.1212	0.2426
22	113.57	0.0088	469.06	0.0021	4.1300	0.2421
23	140.83	0.0071	582.63	0.0017	3.1371	0.2417
24	174.63	0.0057	723.46	0.0014	4.1428	0.2414
25	216.54	0.0046	898.09	0.0011	4.1474	0.2411
26	268.51	0.0037	1114.60	0.0009	4.1511	0.2409
27	332.95	0.0030	1383.10	0.0007	4.1542	0.2407
28	412.86	0.0024	1716.10	0.0006	4.1566	0.2406
29	511.95	0.0020	2129.00	0.0005	4.1585	0.2405
30	634.82	0.0016	2640.90	0.0004	4.1601	0.2404

$$i = 25\%$$

n	caf $(1 + i)^n$	pwf $\dfrac{1}{(1+i)^n}$	uscaf $\dfrac{(1+i)^n - 1}{i}$	ussff $\dfrac{1}{(1+i)^n - 1}$	uspwf $\dfrac{(1+i)^n - 1}{i(1+i)^n}$	uscrf $\dfrac{i(1+i)^n}{(1+i)^n - 1}$
1	1.2500	0.8000	1.0000	1.0000	0.8000	1.2500
2	1.5625	0.6400	2.2500	0.4444	1.4400	0.6944
3	1.9531	0.5120	3.8125	0.2623	1.9520	0.5123
4	2.4414	0.4096	5.7656	0.1734	2.3616	0.4234
5	3.0518	0.3277	8.2070	0.1218	2.6893	0.3718
6	3.8147	0.2621	11.259	0.0888	2.9514	0.3388
7	4.7684	0.2097	15.073	0.0663	3.1611	0.3163
8	5.9605	0.1678	19.842	0.0504	3.3289	0.3004
9	7.4506	0.1342	25.802	0,0388	3.4631	0.2888
10	9.3132	0.1074	33.253	0.0301	3.5705	0.2801
11	11.642	0.0859	42.566	0.0235	3.6564	0.2735
12	14.552	0.0687	54.208	0.0184	3.7251	0.2684
13	18.190	0.0550	68.760	0.0145	3.7801	0.2645
14	22.737	0.0440	86.949	0.0115	3.8241	0.2615
15	28.422	0.0352	109.69	0.0091	3.8593	0.2591
16	35.527	0.0281	138.11	0.0072	3.8874	0.2572
17	44.409	0.0225	173.64	0.0058	3.9099	0.2558
18	55.511	0.0180	218.04	0.0046	3.9279	0.2546
19	69.389	0.0144	273.56	0.0037	3.9424	0.2537
20	86.736	0.0115	342.94	0.0029	3.9539	0.2529
21	108.42	0.0092	429.68	0.0023	3.9631	0.2523
22	135.53	0.0074	538.10	0.0019	3.9705	0.2519
23	219.41	0.0059	673.63	0.0015	3.9764	0.2515
24	211.76	0.0047	843.03	0.0012	3.9811	0.2512
25	264.70	0.0038	1054.80	0.0009	3.9849	0.2509
26	330.87	0.0030	1319.50	0.0008	9.9879	0.2508
27	413.59	0.0024	1650.40	0.0006	3.9903	0.2506
28	516.99	0.0019	2064.00	0.0005	3.9923	0.2505
29	646.23	0.0015	2580.90	0.0004	3.9938	0.2504
30	807.79	0.0012	3227.20	0.0003	3.9950	0.2503

Appendix 2

Depreciation Formulas

There are two most commonly used depreciation formulas. They are:

a. Straight line depreciation

b. Declining balance depreciation

These two types of depreciation will be described in turn below.

a. Straight Line Depreciation

Let P = inital value of asset
R = salvage value
n = useful life in years

Then, the relation of P, R and n can be represented by the following diagram:

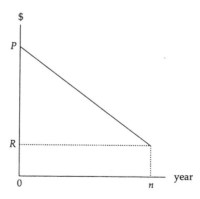

$$\text{Decrease of value in one year} = \frac{P - R}{n}$$

Value at the end of year $k = P - k\dfrac{(P-R)}{n}$,   where $k \leqq n$

b. Declining Balance Depreciation

Similarly, the relation of P, R and n can be represented by the following diagram:

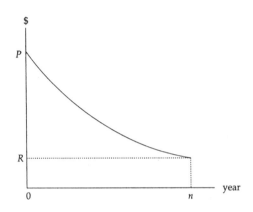

Mathematically, P, R and n are related by:

$R = P(1 - r)^n$

and r $(0 < r < 1)$ can be calculated by the formula itself since R, P and n are known. After r is calculated, the value at the end of year k $(k \leqq n)$ can be known.

Value at the end of year $1 = P(1 - r)$
Value at the end of year $2 = P(1 - r)^2$
.   .
.   .
.   .
Value at the end of year $k = P(1 - r)^k$
.   .
.   .
.   .
Value at the end of year $n = P(1 - r)^n = R$

Appendix 3

IRR — Computer Program Listing

```
10   REM   ******************
20   REM   PROGRAM DESCRIPTION:
30   REM   THIS PROGRAM CALCULATES THE INTERNAL RATE OF
40         RETURN OF A PROJECT CASH FLOW.
50   REM   ******************
60   REM   DATA DICTIONARY:
70   REM
80   REM   INPUT VARIABLES:
90   REM   N            : DURATION OF PROJECT
100  REM   CAPITAL      : INITIAL CAPITAL OUTLAY OF PROJECT
110  REM   MODE$        : MODE OF CASH OUT/CASH IN
120  REM   CASH-OUT     : CASH OUT PER YEAR
130  REM   CASH-IN      : CASH IN PER YEAR
140  REM
150  REM   WORKING/OUTPUT VARIABLES:
160  REM   PWF          : PRESENT WORTH FACTOR
170  REM   NCF          : NET CASH FLOW
180  REM   DCF          : DISCOUNT CASH FLOW
190  REM   TOT. DCF     : TOTAL DISCOUNT CASH FLOW FROM
                          YEAR 1 TO YEAR N
200  REM   I            : DISCOUNTING RATE
210  REM   NPW          : NET PRESENT WORTH
220  REM   IRR          : INTERNAL RATE OF RETURN
230  REM   ******************
240  REM   CONTROL MODULE
250  REM
260  GOSUB 340       : REM   INITIALISE MODULE
270  GOSUB 410       : REM   INPUT DATA MODULE
280  GOSUB 750       : REM   CALCULATION MODULE
290  GOSUB 940       : REM   PRINT MODULE
300  END
```

```
310  REM    ******************
320  REM    INITIALISE MODULE
330  REM
340  DIM I(2), NPW(2), CASH OUT(100), CASH IN(100), PWF(100),
     NCF(100), DCF(100)
350  I(1) = .1
360  I(2) = .15
370  RETURN
380  REM
390  REM    INPUT DATA MODULE
400  REM
410  INPUT "DURATION OF PROJECT IN YEARS (MAX = 100)"; N
420  PRINT
430  INPUT "INITIAL CAPITAL OUTLAY, ie. CASH OUT AT YEAR 0";
     CAPITAL
440  PRINT
450  REM    DATA FOR CASH OUT PER YEAR
460  INPUT "ARE CASH OUTS IN EACH YEARS A CONSTANT AMOUNT
     (Y/N)"; MODES
470  PRINT
480  IF MODES = "Y" THEN 540
490  FOR J = 1 TO N
500  PRINT "ENTER THE CASH OUT IN YEAR"; J: INPUT CASH-OUT (J)
510  NEXT J
520  GOTO 590
530  REM
540  INPUT "ENTER THE CONSTANT CASH OUT PER YEAR";
     CASH-OUT (J)
550  FOR J = 1 TO N
560  CASH-OUT (J) = CASH-OUT
570  NEXT J
580  REM
590  PRINT
600  INPUT "ARE CASH INS IN EACH YEAR A CONSTANT AMOUNT
     (Y/N)"; MODES
610  PRINT '
620  IF MODES = "Y" THEN 680
630  FOR J = 1 TO N
640  PRINT "ENTER THE CASH-IN AT YEAR"; J: INPUT CASH-IN (J)
650  NEXT J
660  GOTO 720
670  REM    CONSTANT CASH IN PER YEAR
680  INPUT "ENTER THE CONSTANT CASH IN PER YEAR"; CASH.IN (J)
690  FOR J = 1 TO N
```

```
700   CASH-IN (J) = CASH-IN
710   NEXT J
720   RETURN
730   REM      **************
740   REM         CALCULATION MODULE
750   FORK = 1 TO 2
760   TOT. DCF = 0
770   FOR J = 1 TO N
780   PWF (J) = 1/(1 + I(K)) ^J
790   NCF (J) = CASH-IN (J) – CASH-OUT (J)
800   DCF (J) = NCF (J) * PWF (J)
810   TOT. DCF = TOT. DCF + DCF (J)
820   NEXT J
830   NPW (K) = TOT. DCF-CAPITAL
840   IF ABS (NPW(K)) < .0001 * CAPITAL THEN IRR = I(K): GOTO 900
850   NEXT K
860   IRR = 1(1) + (NPW(l)/(NPW(l) – NPW(2))) * (I(2) -I(1))
870   I(1) = I(2)
880   I(2) = IRR
890   GOTO 750
900   RETURN
910   REM      *************
920   REM         PRINT MODULE
930   REM
940   PRINT : PRINT : PRINT
950   PRINT TAB(3); "YEAR"; TAB(14); "CASH OUT"; TAB(24); "CASH IN";
960   PRINT TAB(35); "NCF"; TAB(48); "PWF"; TAB(63); "DCF"
970   PRINT TAB(3); "_ _ _"; TAB(14); "_ _ _ _ _ _ _"; TAB(24); "_ _ _ _ _";
980   PRINT TAB(35); "_ _ _"; TAB(48); "_ _ _"; TAB(63); "_ _ _"
990   PRINT
1000  PRINT TAB(5); 0; TAB(15); CAPITAL: TAB(25); 0;
1010  PRINT TAB(35); – CAPITAL; TAB(45); – TAB(60); – CAPITAL
1020  FOR J = 1 TO N
1030  PRINT TAB(5); J; TAB(15); CASH-OUT (J); TAB(25); CASH-IN (J)
1040  PRINT TAB(35); NCF (J); TAB(45); PWF (J); TAB(60); DCF (J)
1050  NEXT J
1060  PRINT TAB(60); "_ _ _ _ _ _ _ _"
1070  PRINT
1080  PRINT TAB(50); "NPW ="; TAB(60); NPW(K)
1090  PRINT TAB(60); "_ _ _ _ _ _ _"
1100  PRINT "ANS: IRR ="; IRR
1110  PRINT
1120  PRINT TAB(20); " * * * * * * * END OF PROGRAM * * * * * *"
1130  RETURN
```